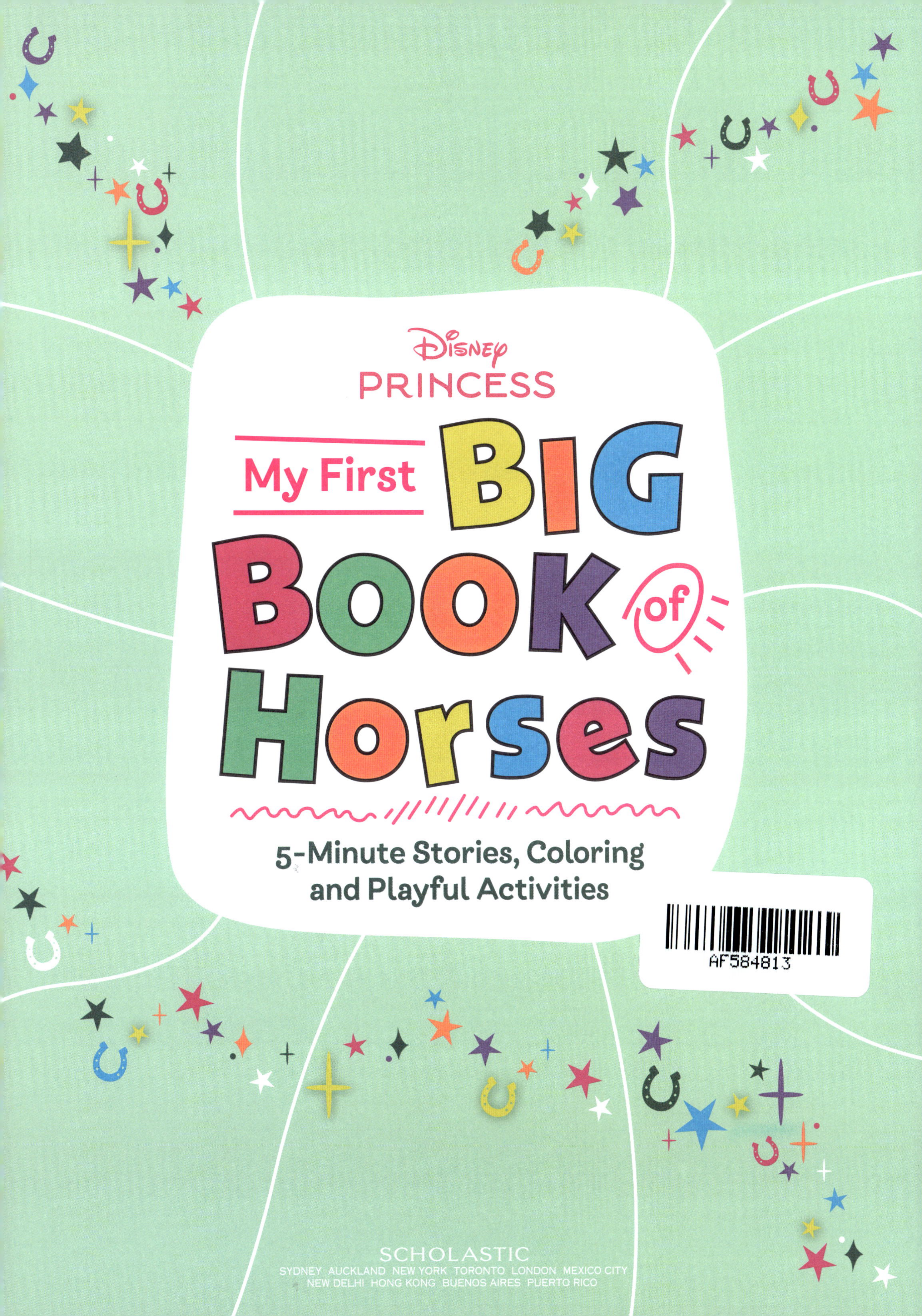
Disney
PRINCESS
My First BIG BOOK of Horses
5-Minute Stories, Coloring and Playful Activities
AF584813
SCHOLASTIC
SYDNEY AUCKLAND NEW YORK TORONTO LONDON MEXICO CITY
NEW DELHI HONG KONG BUENOS AIRES PUERTO RICO

This book belongs to...

(Write **YOUR NAME** here.)

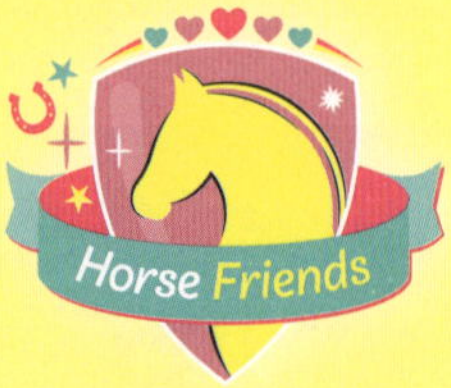
Horse Friends

GET TO KNOW THE HORSES who bring friendship, adventure, and love to the world of the princesses.

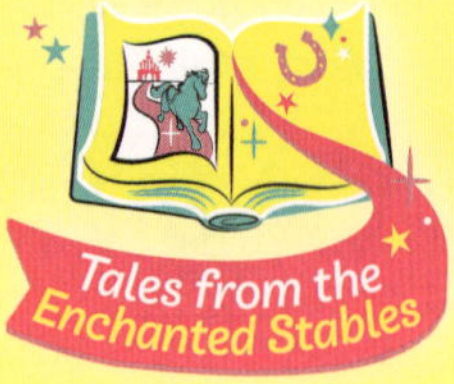
Tales from the Enchanted Stables

READ HEARTWARMING COMIC STORIES and discover the many **ADVENTURES** the princesses and their horses enjoy together.

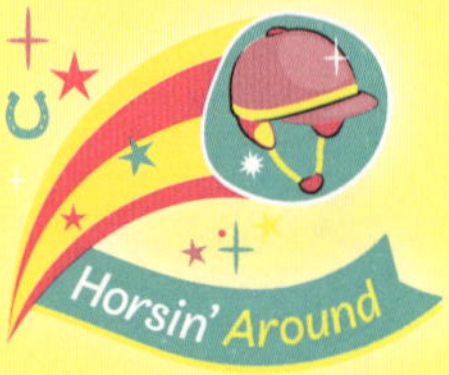
Horsin' Around

Have fun with **GAMES, PUZZLES,** and **ACTIVITIES** starring your favorite horses.

Stables Backstage

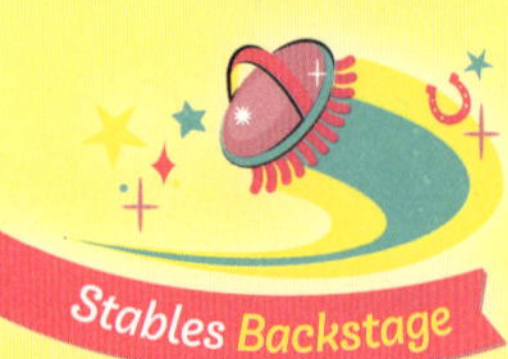

LEARN ABOUT the princesses' **HORSES,** their behaviors and needs, and how to care for them.

Color & Stick

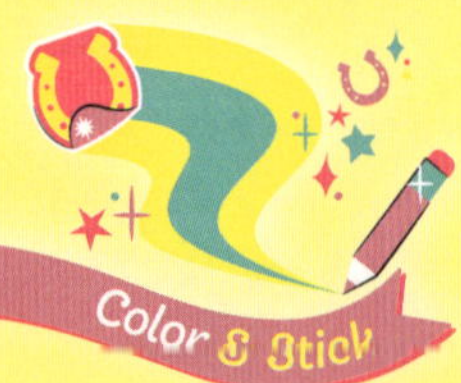

BRING TO LIFE OUTFITS AND EQUIPMENT of Disney Princesses and their horses.

Published by Scholastic Australia in 2026.
Scholastic Australia Pty Limited
PO Box 579 Gosford NSW 2250
ABN 11 000 614 577

ISBN 978-1-76164-749-9

Printed in China.

Content and text by Sally Gilbert
Cover and design by Gaia Daverio
Additional photos © Shutterstock

Meet the princesses and their horses.

What kind of rider are you?

These are Sticker Pages

Ride the Magic!

Before venturing into the pages of this book, **meet** all the Disney Princess horses at their stables. **Read** and **discover** their names, breeds, personalities, and more. Don't forget to **decorate** each stable with a **sticker.**

BREED: Akhal-Teke
PERSONALITY: Loyal, intelligent, courageous
LIKES: Eating straw and relaxing in the sun
DISLIKES: Being in danger and being called a cow or a sheep

BREED: Arabian
PERSONALITY: Feisty, sporty, and intelligent
LIKES: Walking in the desert and playing polo
DISLIKES: Losing a polo match

Merida and...

BREED: Shire horse
PERSONALITY: Brave, stubborn, and loyal
LIKES: Eating oats and galloping down hills at full speed
DISLIKES: Facing bears and having to deal with magic

Aurora and...

BREED: Andalusian
PERSONALITY: Athletic, proud, and brave
LIKES: Eating strawberries, listening to Aurora's singing, and jousting
DISLIKES: Facing fires or thorns and tumbling into water

Snow White and...

BREED: Oldenburg
PERSONALITY: Kind, faithful, and clever
LIKES: Walking in the woods and jumping
DISLIKES: Snow White or the Prince being in danger

BREED: Lipizzaner
PERSONALITY: Brave, determined, and bold
LIKES: Eating apples and investigating with Rapunzel
DISLIKES: Being bothered by mosquitoes and being outsmarted

BREED: Egyptian Arabian
PERSONALITY: Kind, intelligent, and patient
LIKES: Listening to Ariel's singing while walking along the beach
DISLIKES: Ariel brushing the seaweed out of her tail or mane

BREED: Belgian draft horse
PERSONALITY: Strong, loyal, and caring
LIKES: Going on adventures with Belle
DISLIKES: Facing wolves and traveling dark spooky roads

BREED: Selle Français
PERSONALITY: Kind, smart, and loyal
LIKES: Being with his castle friends
DISLIKES: Anyone being treated badly by others

BREED: Thoroughbred
PERSONALITY: Clever, full of energy, and high-spirited
LIKES: Trotting along in search of new flavors
DISLIKES: Being spooked by sudden noises and movements

Are you ready to **ride** with the Disney Princesses and their horse friends? Turn the page to **discover everything about** their special bond and the **adventures** and **activities** they **enjoy** together!

Khan and Mulan

Khan is the Fa family horse and is **very loyal** to Mulan. He is **intelligent** and **courageous**, with great **physical strength**, which he shows on his many adventures with Mulan.

Khan the Akhal-Teke

ORIGIN: These horses have been bred for over 3,000 years. They are a descendant of the **Turkoman horse**, known and valued especially in China.

FEATURES: They have long **narrow heads** and **necks**, hooded or almond-shaped eyes, and a distinctive **shiny coat**.

ATTITUDE: Akhal-Teke horses are strong, resilient, and **agile**, but also **obedient** and eager to learn. In the past they were **war horses**, but today they are perfect for all equestrian disciplines.

Mulan and Khan are setting off to search for a friend who is lost. Can you tell who the friend is by **matching** their **shadow?**

Cri-Kee

Mushu

Little Brother

Color in the blank parts to complete the picture. **Use** this picture to **guide** you.

Solution

Little Brother

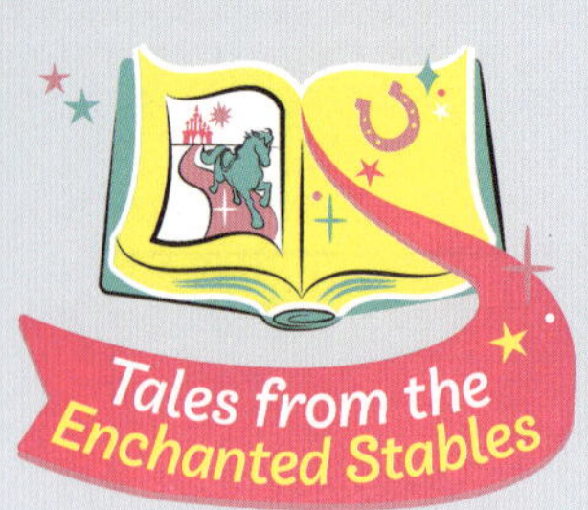

Where Is Little Brother?

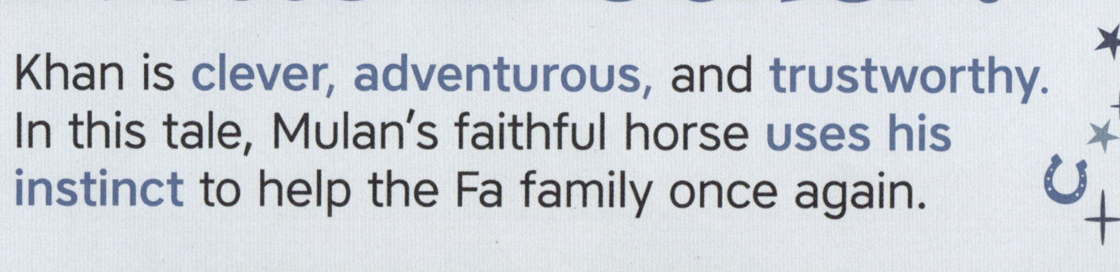

Khan is clever, adventurous, and trustworthy. In this tale, Mulan's faithful horse uses his instinct to help the Fa family once again.

Script: Harriet Webster for Book on a Tree; layout: Benedetta Barone; cleanup: Manuela Razzi; color: Maawillustration; lettering: Francesca Paglialunga for Studio RAM; comics editing: Elena Galli

LITTLE BROTHER!

CLIP
CLOP

WHY ARE YOU SLOWING DOWN, KHAN?

WHAT IS IT?

OOF!

DID YOU HEAR SOMETHING, KHAN?
BRRH!
THUD THUD

OKAY, LET'S BE ON THE LOOKOUT FOR DANGER...

AROOO!
WHAT WAS THAT? A WOLF?!

KHAN! WHY ARE YOU RUNNING SO FAST?!
THUD THUD
THUD THUD

OH MY!
RUFF RUFF

HEY, LITTLE BROTHER!

WHAT HAVE YOU GOT THERE?
RUFF RUFF

HERE YOU GO, YOU SILLY DOG.

WELL DONE, KHAN. NOW LET'S GO HOME!

BACK AT THE VILLAGE...
WELCOME BACK HOME, LITTLE ONE!
RUFF RUFF

THAT SOUNDS LIKE...

LITTLE BROTHER!
HOW DID YOU FIND HIM, MULAN?

The End

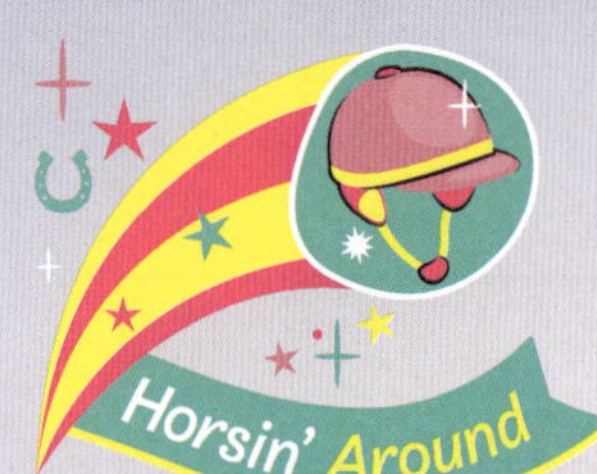

Avalanche Escape

Khan certainly has the speed and endurance for riding in the snowy mountains, but it can be dangerous! Race Mulan and Khan along the trail as quickly as you can to escape the avalanche!

Stick

Stick

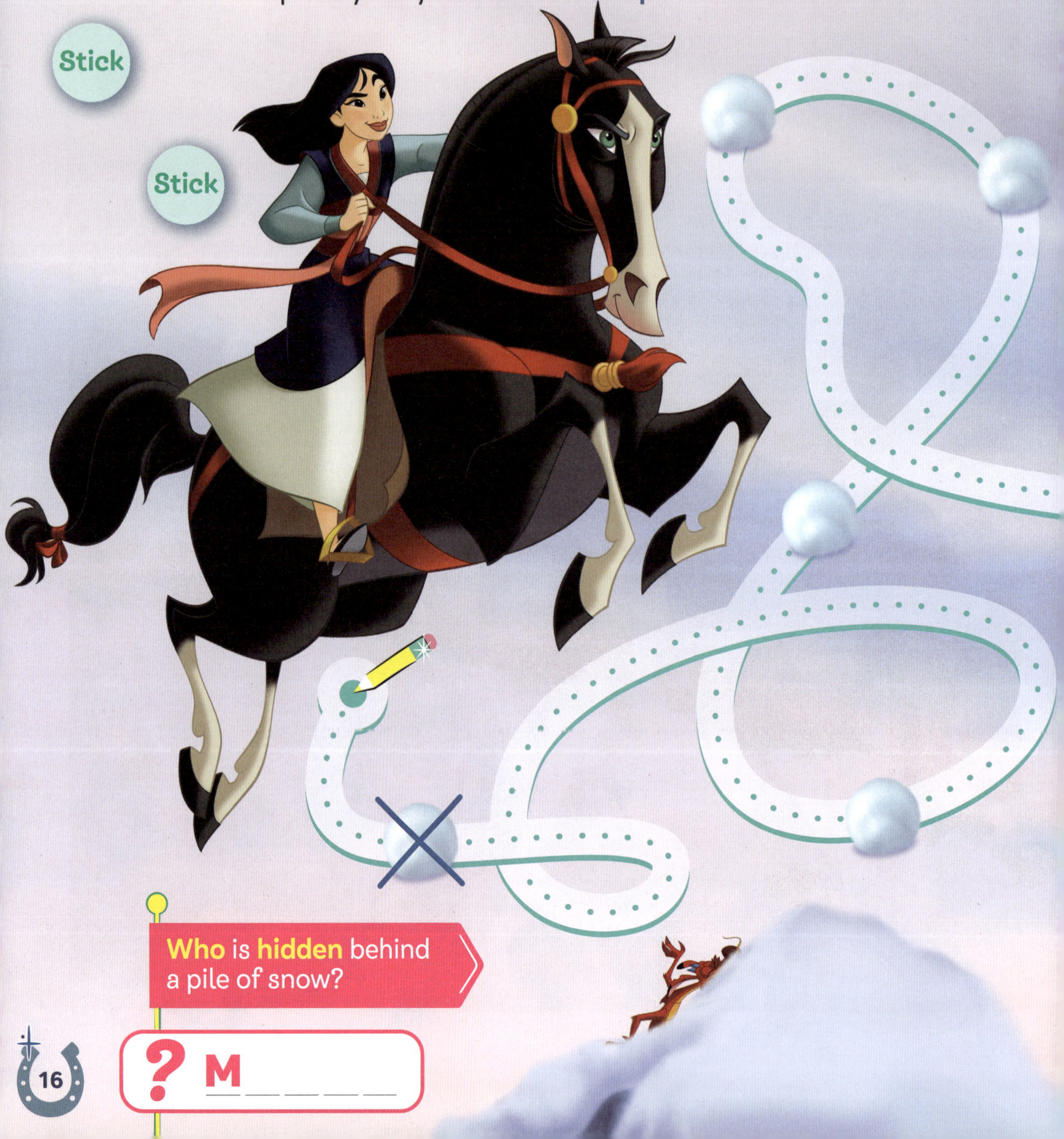

Who is hidden behind a pile of snow?

? M _ _ _ _ _

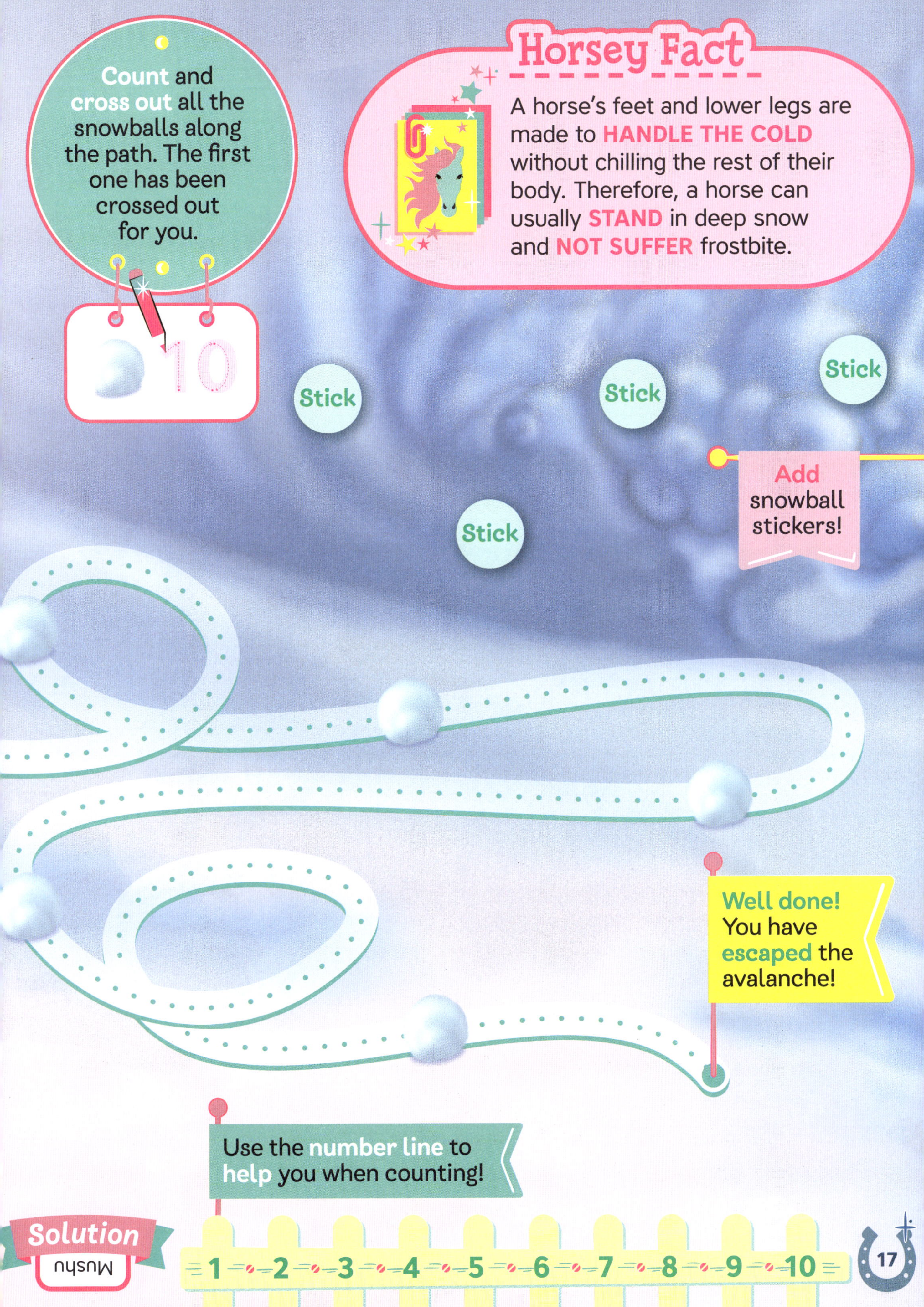
Count and cross out all the snowballs along the path. The first one has been crossed out for you.
10
Horsey Fact
A horse's feet and lower legs are made to HANDLE THE COLD without chilling the rest of their body. Therefore, a horse can usually STAND in deep snow and NOT SUFFER frostbite.
Stick
Stick
Stick
Stick
Add snowball stickers!
Well done! You have escaped the avalanche!
Use the number line to help you when counting!
Solution
Mushu
1 2 3 4 5 6 7 8 9 10

Horse-Care Routine!

Taking care of a horse is a **big challenge.** Look at all the activities Mulan has **planned** at Khan's stable!

1

LOOK at Khan's horsey gear that needs to be removed once at the stable, and **TRACE** the name of each item.

Saddle

Bridle

Blanket

This is a Sticker Page
2
PUT these horseshoes IN SIZE ORDER, starting with the smallest.
A
B
C
D
D, , ,
3
STICK the hay in a neat pile.
Stick
4
CROSS OUT the bucket with a HOLE in it.
A
B
C
D
E
Solutions
2 - D, B, A, C
4 - B
19

Nura and Jasmine

Nura is a **highly spirited** horse, and Jasmine is the only person at the Sultan's palace who has been able to tame her. Nura and Jasmine **share a love of polo** and they **make a great team**!

Nura the Arabian

ORIGIN: The Arabian horse is one of the **oldest breeds** in the world. It dates back 4,000 years to the **Arabian Peninsula,** from which it takes its name.

FEATURES: Arabian horses have a **shorter back** to help them be **lighter** and **glide across the sand**.

ATTITUDE: They **tolerate the heat** well. In the past they lived next to their owners' tents and traveled across the desert. Known for their **speed** and **endurance,** they need an experienced master.

Color in the blank parts to complete the picture. **Use** this picture to **guide** you.

It's a beautiful day for a polo match! **Look closely** at the picture and **count the birds flying** in the sky!

1 2 3 4 5 6 7 8 9 10

Use the **number line** to **help** you when counting!

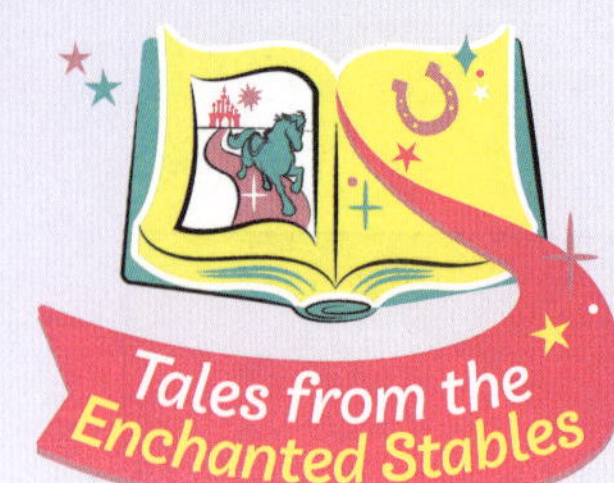

The Night Ride

Nura is **determined**, **sturdy**, and **light** on her feet, which is very useful indeed when she is about to **embark** on a **desert adventure** with Jasmine, especially at **night**.

Script: Harriet Webster for Book on a Tree; layout: Veronica Di Lorenzo; cleanup: Marino Gentile; color: Maawillustration; lettering: Maurizio Clausi for Symmaceo; comics editing: Valentina Cambi

AT THE DUNES...
LOOK AT THE SKY!

WOW, IT IS SO BEAUTIFUL!

WHOOSH!

BUT SUDDENLY...
WATCH OUT, NURA. THE WIND IS PICKING UP!
WHOOOSH!
NEIGH!

WHOOSH!

WHOOSH!
OH, NO!
THUD!

COUGH! COUGH!
ACHOO!

WHERE ARE WE?

WHICH WAY SHOULD WE GO?

LATER...
I THINK WE ARE...

... LOST!

!

WHOA, NURA!

IT'S CARPET!

FLAP
FLAP
HEY! DID YOU FOLLOW US?

AHA!

LET'S GO HOME!

The End

Desert Ride!

Jasmine and Nura are going for a magical nighttime ride across the sand dunes! Follow the path and answer the questions along the way.

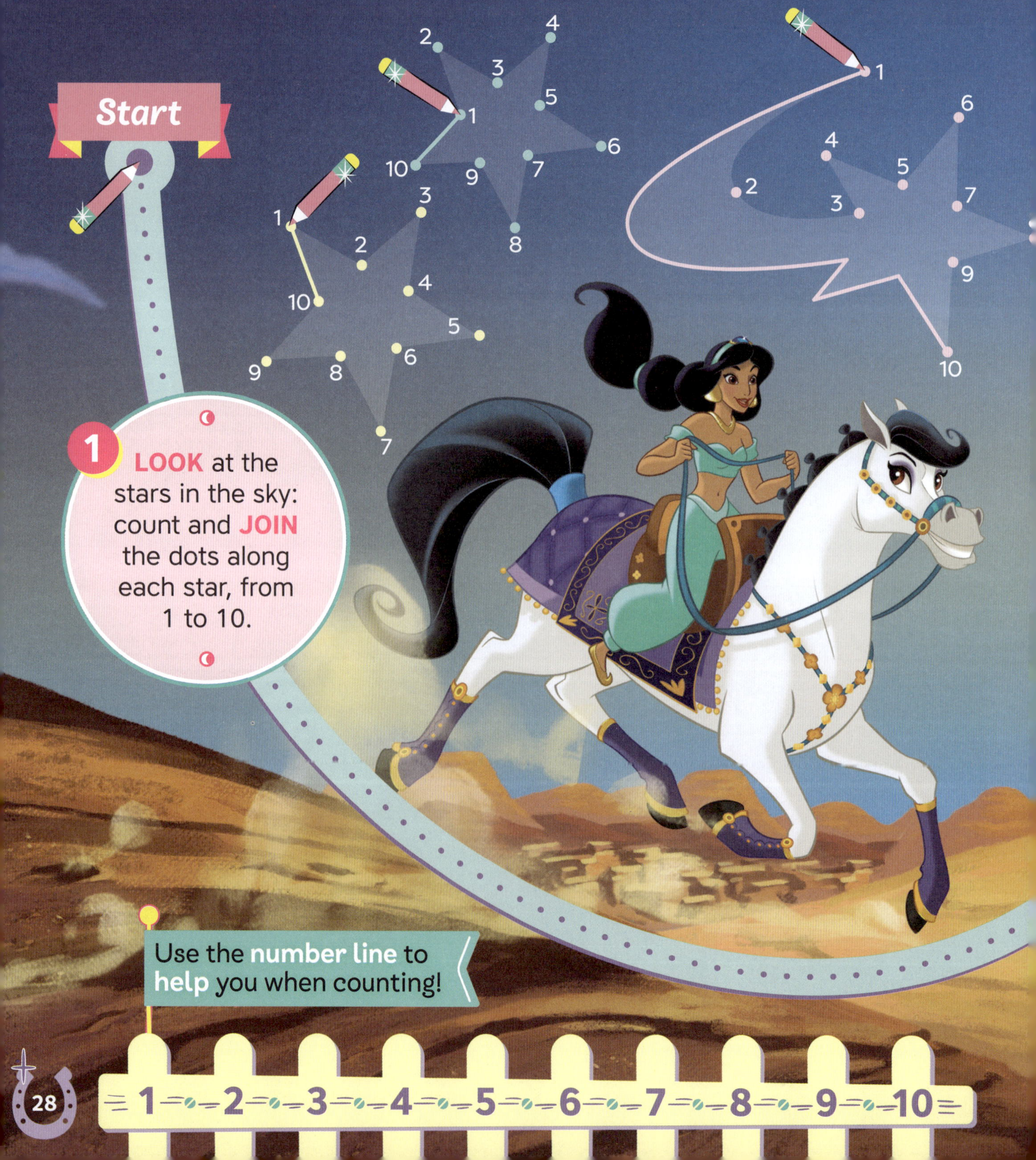

Start

1 **LOOK** at the stars in the sky: count and **JOIN** the dots along each star, from 1 to 10.

Use the **number line** to **help** you when counting!

1 2 3 4 5 6 7 8 9 10

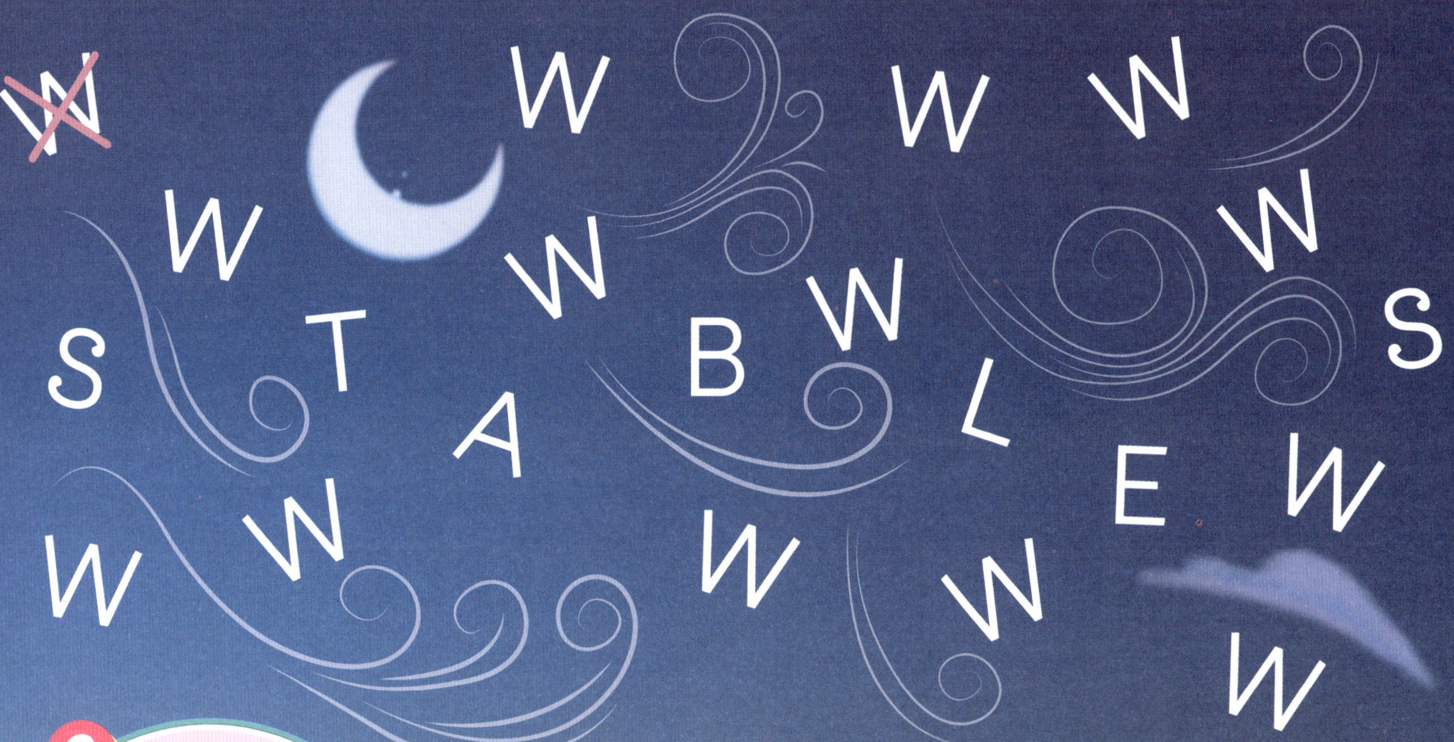

~~W~~ W W W W W W W S T B S L A E W W W W W W

2 It's a very windy ride! **CROSS OUT** every ***W*** letter and **READ** where Jasmine and Nura are going next.

3 **DRAW A LINE** from each piece to its correct place to **REASSEMBLE** the image of Carpet!

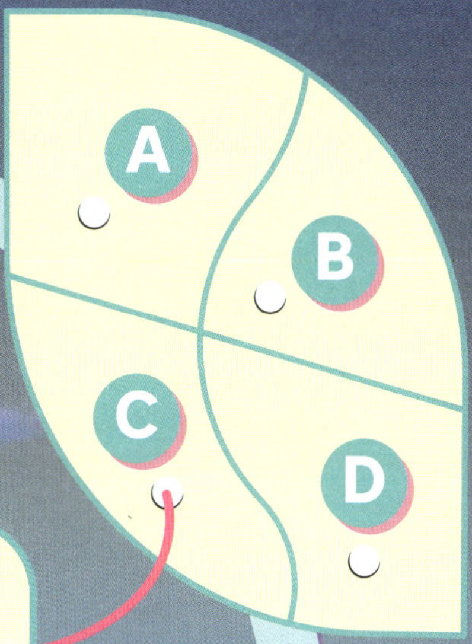

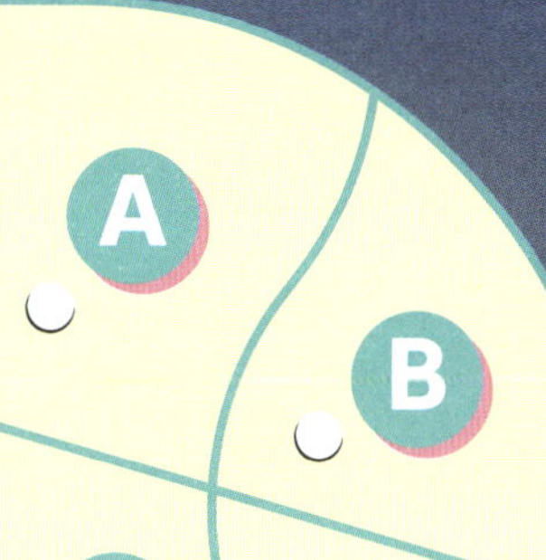

Finish

Solutions

2 - STABLES
3 - 1—C, 2—A, 3—B, 4—D

A Visit from the Vet

Jasmine has **called out** the royal vet to get Nura **checked** over after their challenging desert ride. **Read** and **carry out** the steps the vet took to **examine** her!

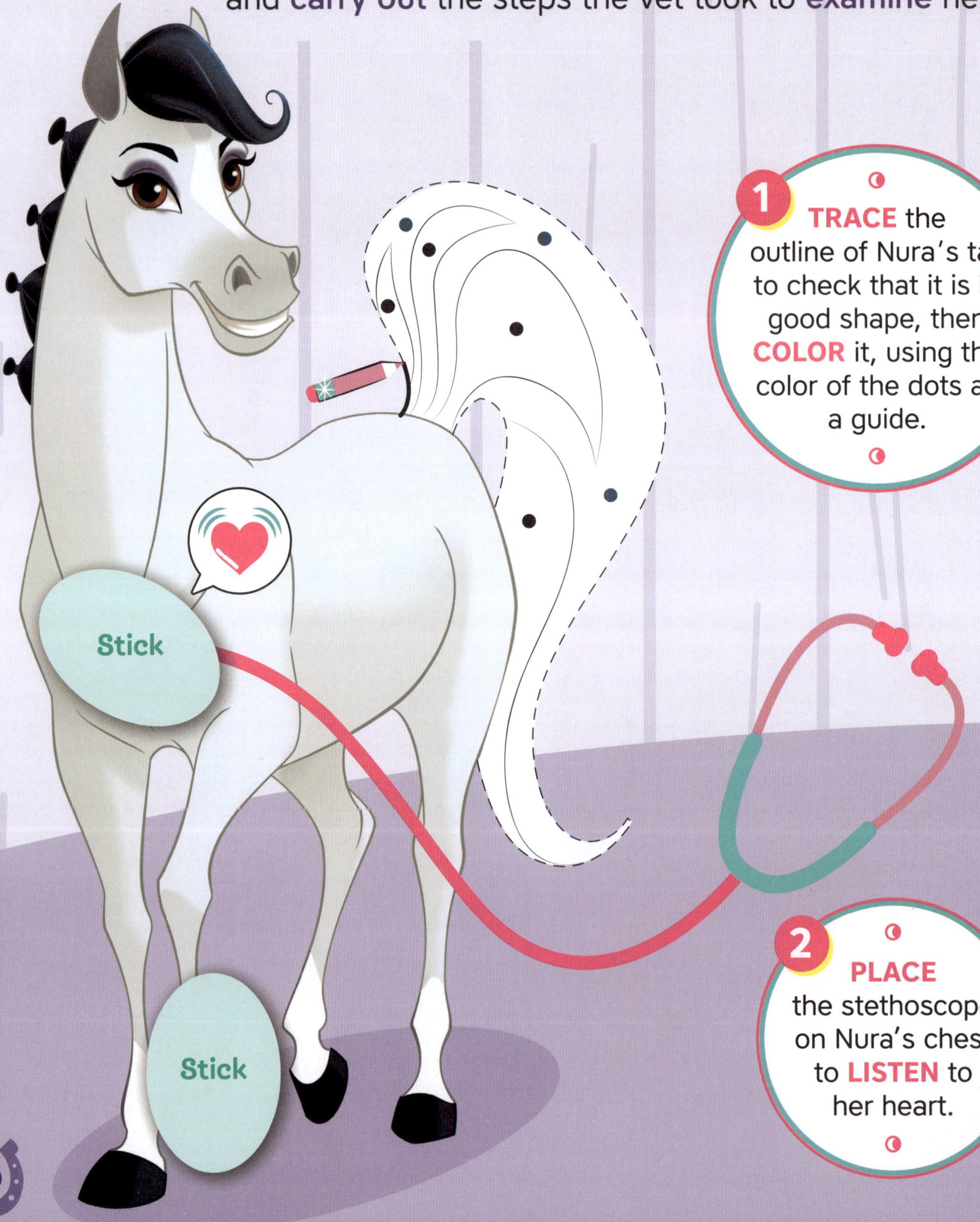

Stick

Stick

1 **TRACE** the outline of Nura's tail to check that it is in good shape, then **COLOR** it, using the color of the dots as a guide.

2 **PLACE** the stethoscope on Nura's chest to **LISTEN** to her heart.

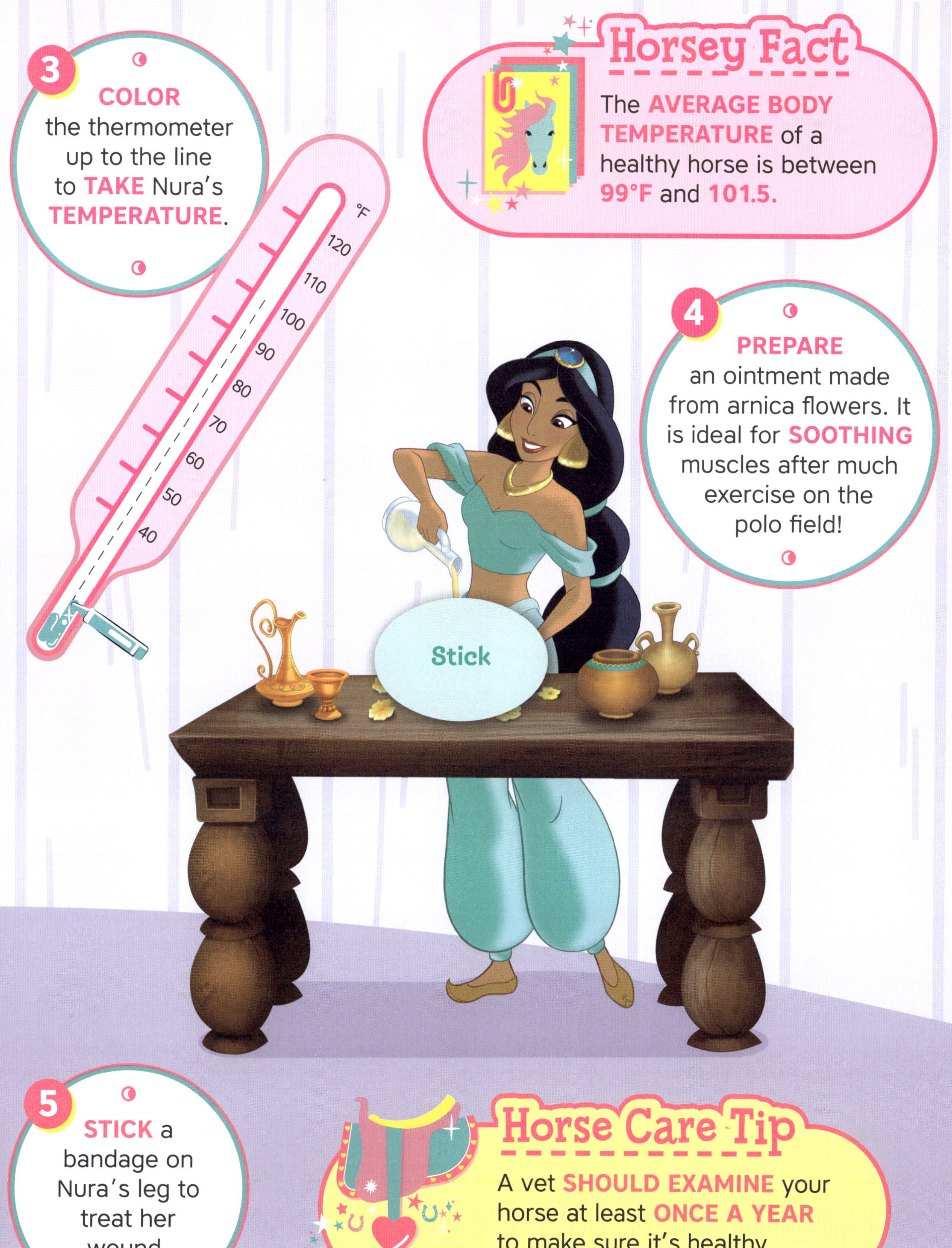

3

COLOR the thermometer up to the line to **TAKE** Nura's **TEMPERATURE**.

Horsey Fact

The **AVERAGE BODY TEMPERATURE** of a healthy horse is between **99°F** and **101.5.**

4

PREPARE an ointment made from arnica flowers. It is ideal for **SOOTHING** muscles after much exercise on the polo field!

5

STICK a bandage on Nura's leg to treat her wound.

Horse Care Tip

A vet **SHOULD EXAMINE** your horse at least **ONCE A YEAR** to make sure it's healthy.

Angus and Merida

Angus is **powerful**, **clever**, and **loyal**. He is Merida's most **trusted confidant** and she allows no one else in the castle to see to his care.

Angus the Shire Horse

ORIGIN: Shire horses descend from the medieval war horse called the English Great Horse. The name refers to the **English shire** where the breed was developed (Lincolnshire and Cambridgeshire).

FEATURES: They are usually black, bay, brown, or gray in color, with feathered legs. They are known for being the **tallest horses** in the world and they are also incredibly **strong**.

ATTITUDE: Shire horses are easygoing, **calm**, and **patient**. They are noble and hardworking, too.

Can you **find** Angus's **hairbrush** hidden on the page?

Color in the blank parts to complete the picture. **Use** this picture to **guide** you.

Solution

Clever Angus!

Merida and **Angus** have a strong and **loving bond.** Merida can often coax Angus into their next adventure, even when it is very early.

Script: Harriet Webster for Book on a Tree; layout and clean.jp: Benedetta Barone; color: Maawillustration; lettering: Studio RAM, Bologna

SOON AFTER...
WE'LL EAT LATER!
RUMBLE!

SO LATE...

I THINK THIS IS A SHORTCUT!

LATER...
I DON'T REMEMBER THIS BIT...

NOT NOW, ANGUS!
CHOMP CHOMP!

NGGGH! WE MUST FOCUS!

WE ARE LOST!

SNIFF! SNIFF!

CLIP
CLOP

HMM... IS THAT SMOKE?!

OH, CLEVER ANGUS!

AT LAST...
NICE TO SEE YOU, MERIDA!
CLIP
CLOP

SNIFF! SNIFF!
I WOKE YOU UP TWICE.
I OVERSLEPT!

I GOT LOST...
DON'T WORRY, LASS, YOU DID NOT MISS ANYTHING!

BUT ANGUS SMELLED SMOKE!
NO, HE SMELLED BREAKFAST! SWEET CHESTNUTS!

A LITTLE LATER...
WELL DONE, MERIDA!
THWANG!
HERE YOU GO, ANGUS!

The End

These are **Sticker Pages**

A Winning Costume

Merida has entered Angus into a **pet costume** competition at the Scottish Highlands festival, where they are hoping to **win the trophy**.

1 **STICK ON** the correct pieces of tartan, then **CONNECT** them to Angus to **DRAPE** them over him.

2 **TRACE OVER** and then **COLOR IN** the antlers as a finishing touch!

Horsey Fact

The United States of America celebrates a national **DRESS UP YOUR PET DAY** on January 14.

3

POINT to who you think deserves to **WIN** the trophy!

4

FIND the trophy on the **STICKER SHEET** to **AWARD** the best costume yourself!

Solutions

1 - 1—B, 2—D, 3—A, 4—C

Free to Roam

Angus loves to **run free** with other horses across the Scottish Highlands. He **gallops** for miles around, which makes him and Merida extremely **happy**.

Which **trail** should Merida take so Angus **can ride** with another companion?

A

B

C

Start

Finish

Wild horses often **live in groups**. **Trace** the **dotted lines** with a pencil to **discover** what a group of horses is **called**.

Herd

Solution

A

Cozy Time

Merida and Angus love **spending quality time** together! Even if it means sharing a **cozy story** in the stables when it is too wet to go riding outside.

Can you **spot** the six changes to **picture B?**

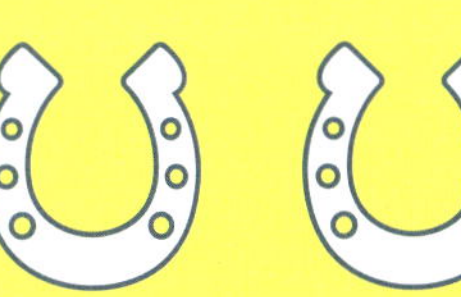

Color in a horseshoe as you **spot** each one.

Horsey Fact

Horses can **UNDERSTAND** several words if **TRAINED**, like ***WALK***, ***WAIT***, ***STAND***, and ***OVER***, to name a few.

Samson and Aurora

Samson is a **kind** and **generous** horse and he often takes Aurora to **visit** the good fairies, Fauna, Flora, and Merryweather at their charming little cottage in the forest.

Samson the Andalusian

ORIGIN: The Andalusian breed comes from the region of **Andalusia,** which is an area in southern **Spain.**

FEATURES: These horses are usually **medium** in size, with a **muscular** but **lean** body. They can **move quickly** and **elegantly**. They are often chosen for parades because of their **beautiful** and **confident** look.

ATTITUDE: They are **smart** and extremely **quick to learn**. This makes them perfect for **dressage** events, because they can learn the steps easily.

Which of these **birds** is **the one** in the scene?

A

B

C

Color in the blank parts to complete the picture. **Use** this picture to **guide** you.

Solution

B

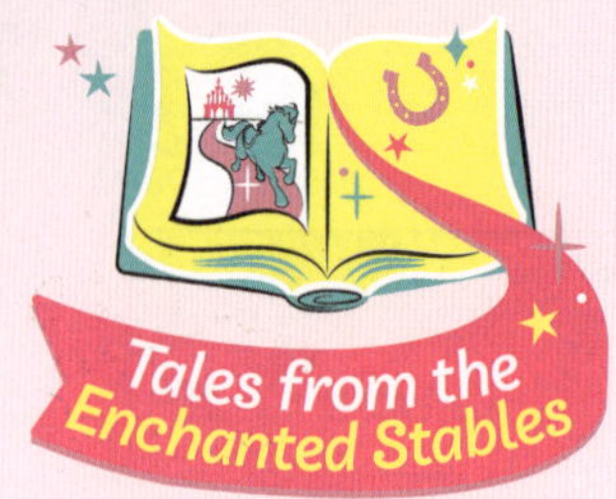

Detective Samson

Samson proves just how **clever** he can be when he and Aurora **help Fauna** out with a little wand trouble. Let's **join** the two friends as they set off on their journey!

Script: Harriet Webster for Book on a Tree; layout: Marino Gentile; cleanup: Benedetta Barone; color: Maawillustration; lettering: Francesca Paglialunga for Studio RAM; comics editing: Elena Galli

FAUNA!
AURORA, DEAR! I LOST MY WAND!
UH-OH!

WHAT IF SOMEONE OR SOMETHING FINDS IT?

WE WILL FIND IT!

BUT I HAVE LOOKED EVERYWHERE ALREADY...
LET US HELP YOU!

THE SEARCH BEGINS...
DID YOU LOOK DOWN HERE?

YES.

UP HERE?
YES.

WHAT ABOUT...

!

HELLO, LITTLE ONE!

... BUT THE WAND IS NOWHERE TO BE FOUND.
HMM...

SNIFF

CHOMP
CHOMP

AHA!

MY WAND!

THANK YOU, DETECTIVE SAMSON!
HE-HE!

The End

Detective Trail

Samson really enjoyed **playing detective** with Aurora while they tried to **uncover the mystery** of Fauna's lost wand. What a **magical team!** Complete these activities inspired by the story.

1. **PEER** into this bird's nest. **HOW MANY EGGS** are there? **TRACE** the number in the box.

2. **POINT** to the **BIGGEST** rose.

Horsey Fact

Horses **LOVE** to eat **FRUITS** like apples, apricots, and cherries! But they should **NEVER EAT** the leaves and seeds of these fruits, because they will make them **VERY SICK**.

3 **LOOK** into this **HOLE**. Who **LIVES** there?

- An owl
- A rabbit

4 **COLOR** these **STRAWBERRIES** to make them extra delicious. What is **HIDING** among them?

Solutions

2. The third one 3. A rabbit
4. A ladybug

Dress Samson!

Aurora has decided to **dress Samson** in beautiful orange accessories today! Doesn't he look **charming?**

A

B

A Perfect Royal Outfit

Aurora and Samson are ready to enter a **royal parade,** and they **look flawless!**

Add stickers as a finishing touch!

Check off the details in Aurora's dress. One doesn't belong!

Solution

C doesn't belong

Astor and Snow White

Astor is **calm, cheerful,** and **giving.** Snow White and Astor simply adore **relaxing together** among all the beautiful, sweet-smelling flowers in the forest glades.

Astor the Oldenburg

ORIGIN: The breeding of these horses started in the 16th century in the city of Oldenburg, in **Northern Germany**.

FEATURES: Oldenburg horses are **tall**, **powerful**, and **muscular**, with **kind eyes** and a **large head**.

ATTITUDE: They are **friendly** and **sweet**, with an air of **nobility**. They have excellent jumping ability and are **enthusiastic** and **energetic**, which makes them **perfect sport horses**.

Snow White is making a flower headdress for Astor. Can you **match** these flowers into **pairs?**

A B C D

1 2 3 4

Solutions

A–3, B–4, C–2, D–1

Color in the blank parts to complete the picture. **Use** this picture to **guide** you.

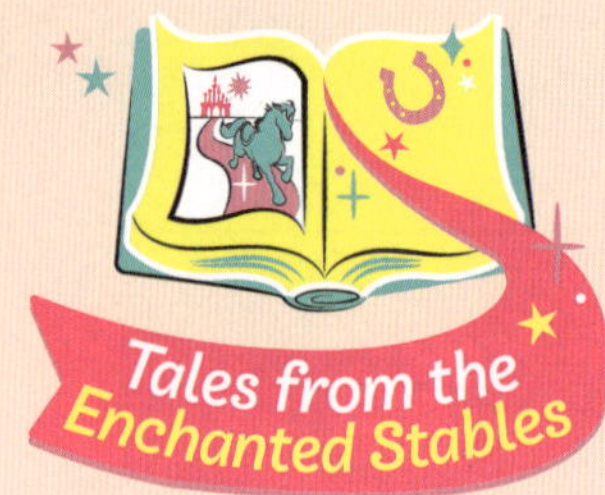

Well Done, Astor!

Astor has a sweet nature, and during this outing he **proves himself** to be a **very kind** and **caring** friend. Join Astor and Snow White as they set off into the **forest**.

Script: Harriet Webster for Book on a Tree; layout: Veronica Di Lorenzo; cleanup: Marco Palazzolo; color: Maawillustration; lettering: Francesca Paglialunga for Studio RAM; comics editing: Elena Galli

WHAT IS THE MATTER?
NEIGH?!
STOMP

COO
COO
COO
WHAT HAVE YOU FOUND?

OH!

COO
COO

COO
A PIGEON!

FLAP
FLAP

WAIT... IT IS A CARRIER PIGEON!

NOW, IF YOU DO NOT MIND, BIRDY...

... LET'S READ THIS NOTE.

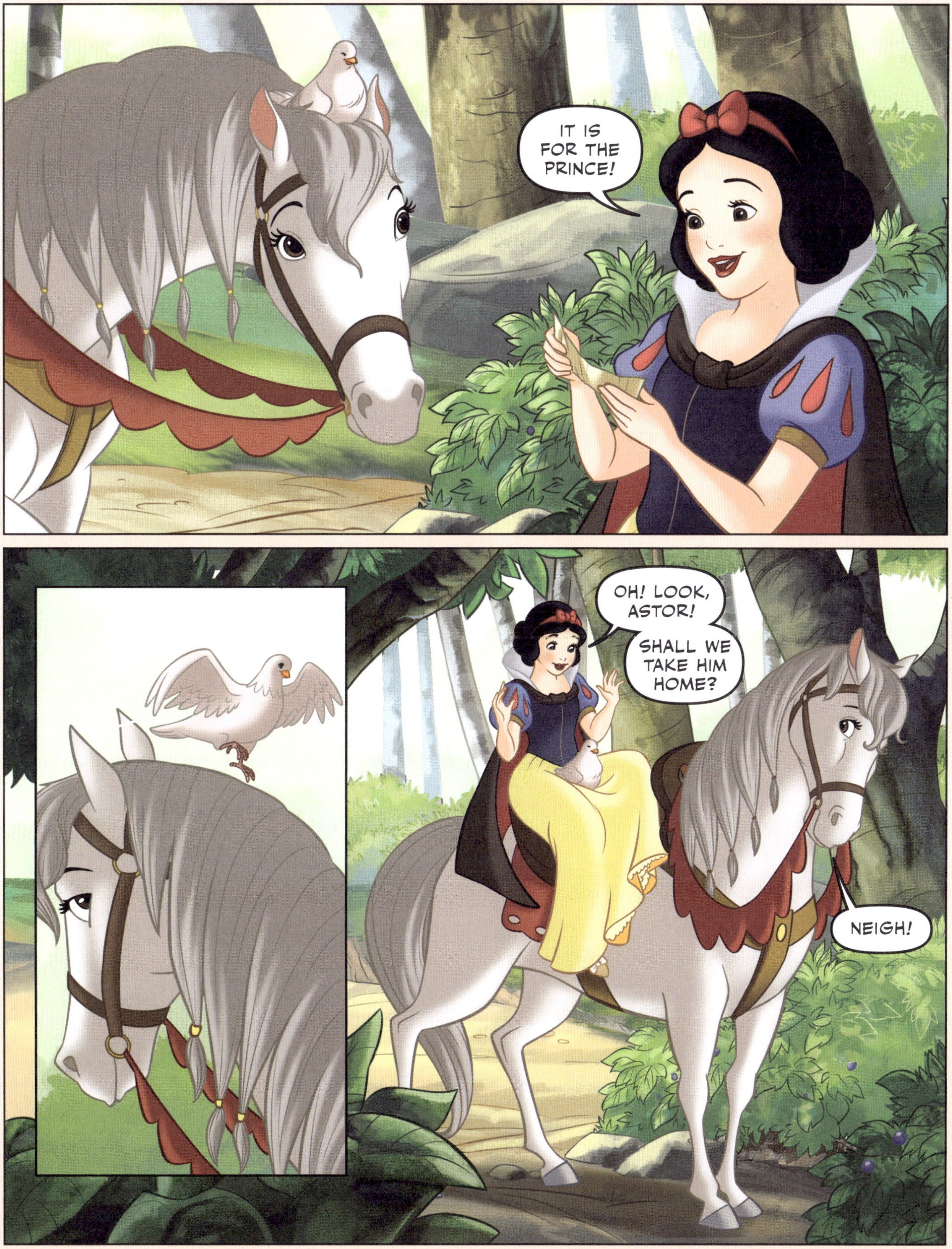

OH! LOOK, ASTOR!

SHALL WE TAKE HIM HOME?

NEIGH!

READY, ASTOR?
NEIGH!
TAP-TAP

ONWARD!
CLOP
CLOP

LATER...
HOME, SWEET HOME!

The End

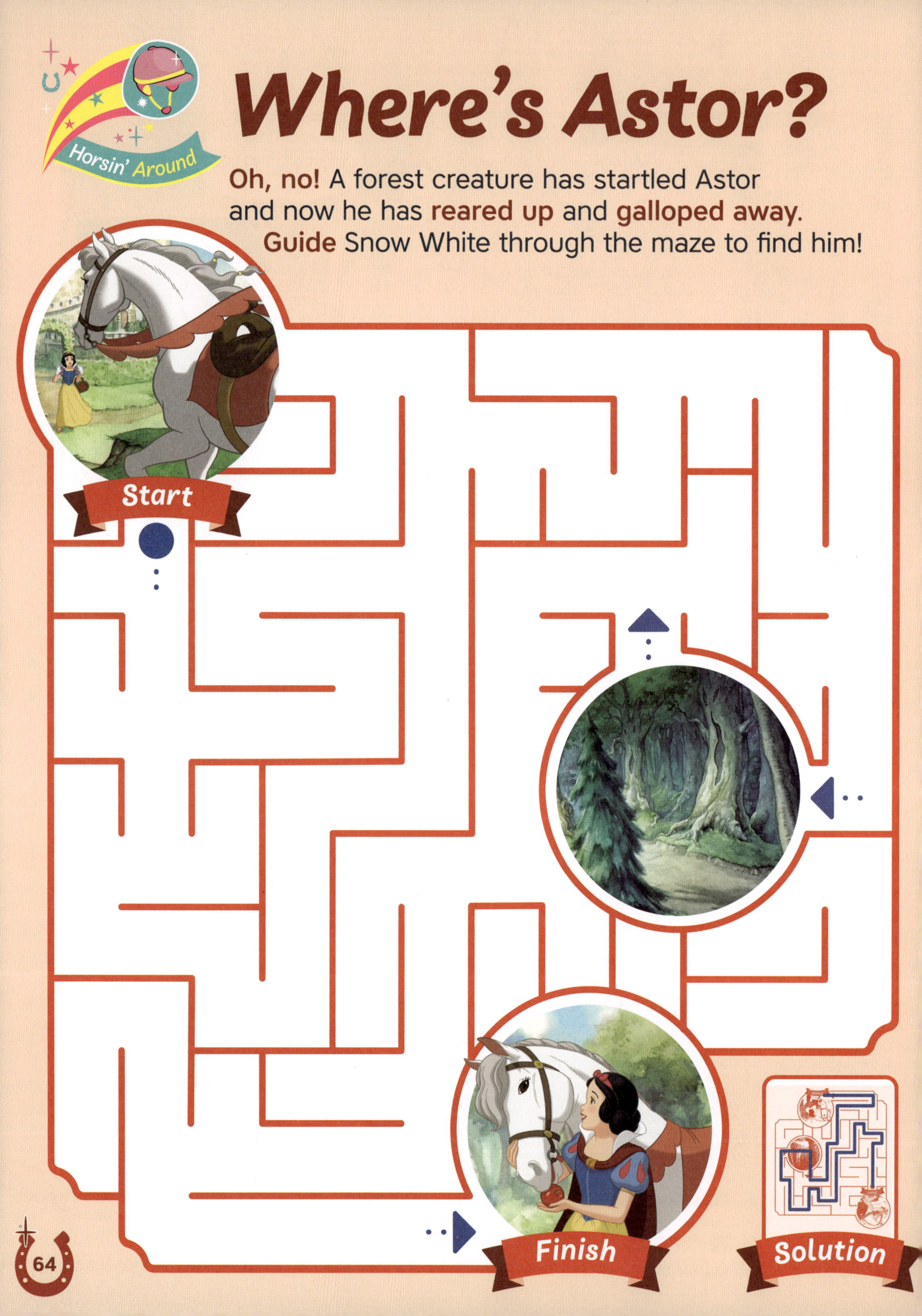

Where's Astor?

Oh, no! A forest creature has startled Astor and now he has **reared up** and **galloped away**. **Guide** Snow White through the maze to find him!

Riding Style

Snow White and Astor are **riding back** to the palace after their heartwarming adventure. What a **perfect day** of riding and friendship for these dear friends!

Draw a line from each **jigsaw piece** to the right place in the picture to **complete** this happy scene.

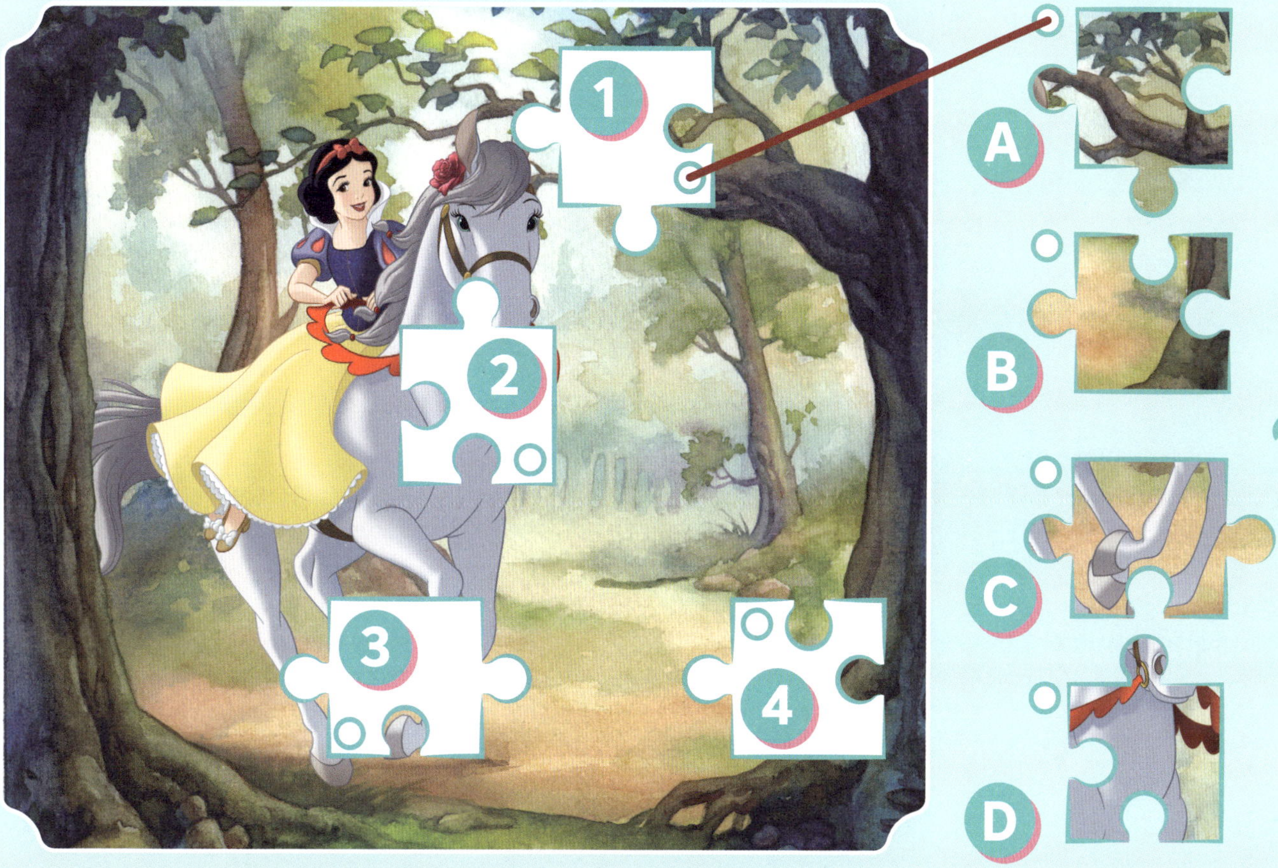

1 2 3 4

A B C D

Snow White's style of riding is **called...**

sidesaddle.

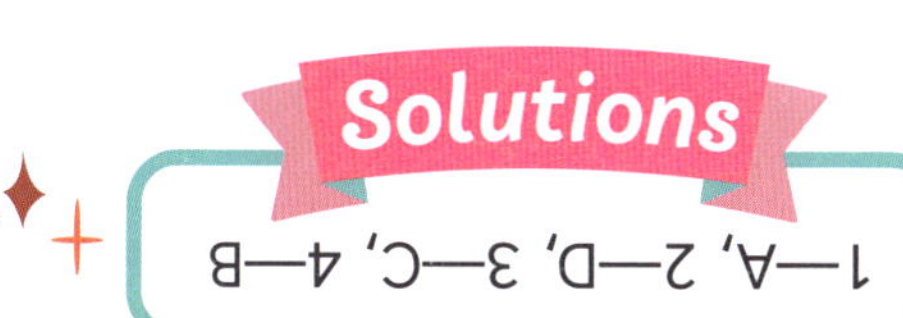

Horsey Fact

For **SIDESADDLE RIDING,** a special saddle allows the rider to sit with **BOTH LEGS ON ONE SIDE** of the horse rather than **ASTRIDE,** which means with one leg on each side of the horse.

Whistle While You Work!

Snow White is spending the day **tidying up** the tack room at the castle stables. She also gets to spend some more **quality time** with Astor!

Look carefully at the tack room. **Stick** in the missing items. Then **draw lines** to place them on Shelf A. **Use** Shelf B to guide you.

Horsey Fact

Many stables keep saddles, bridles, and other riding gear in a **TACK ROOM.** The word *tack* relates to any **OBJECT** that is **USED BY THE RIDER** or horse.

Solutions

A
B
Stick
Stick
Stick
Stick
Stick
This is a Sticker Page

Maximus and Rapunzel

Maximus is **adventurous, courageous,** and **strong,** just like Rapunzel. No wonder they are firm friends! Rapunzel and Maximus love to **ride together** and **be free.**

Maximus the Lipizzaner

ORIGIN: Lipizzaners were first born **more than 400 years ago** in what is today called **Slovenia,** near Northern Italy, in the village of **Lipica**. Hence the breed's name.

FEATURES: They have a **long head** with a **prominent nose**. Their **tail** is carried high and well set.

ATTITUDE: Lipizzaners are renowned for being **elegant** in appearance, **powerful,** and **easily** taught.

Where are the friends going on their ride? **Unscramble** the letters to find out. **Write** your answer in the space below.

E H T D O S W O

T _ _ W _ _ _ _ _

Color in the blank parts to complete the picture. **Use** this picture to **guide** you.

Solution

THE WOODS

A Sweet Victory

Maximus uses his **strength, speed,** and **agility** in this adventure to ensure that he and Rapunzel work as a team to come out on top once again!

Script: Harriet Webster for Book on a Tree; layout: Benedetta Barone; cleanup: Marino Gentile; color: Dario Calabria, Maawillustration; lettering: Maurizio Clausi (Symmaceo)

SOON...
IT IS COMING FROM THERE!
CRASH!
THE SNUGGLY DUCKLING

AT THE SNUGGLY DUCKLING PUB...
HOORAY!
WHAT ARE THEY DOING?

CHARGE!
SWISH!

YAY!
WHAT FUN!
ATTILA AND DAISY WIN THE MATCH!

WHO WILL FACE ME NEXT?

NOBODY?
HOLD ON! WHERE IS MAX?
BONG!
BING!
BANG!

NOT FAR...
COME ON, MAX!

I KNOW YOU LOVE APPLES...
BUT WE CAN WIN!

MOMENTS LATER...
ARE YOU READY?!

GRRR!
GO!!!

CHARGE!

HURRR?!

PUTT!
PUTT!
PUTT!
PUTT!
PUTT!

OUCH!
WHACK!

RAPUNZEL AND MAX...
ARE THE **WINNERS** OF THE PAN TOURNAMENT!

WELL DONE, MAX!

BACK AT THE STABLES...

YOU WERE GREAT, MAX!

OH, I ALMOST FORGOT...
TO GIVE YOU THE OTHER PRIZE!
NEIGH!

WHAT WOULD I DO WITHOUT YOU?

The End

Maximus Portrait!

Rapunzel has **portrayed** Maximus in a picture to hang in her room. It reminds her of all the **wonderful times** they have **shared together** and what a **trusted friend** he is.

Can you **find** the **six differences** between portraits A and B?

Stables Backstage
Happy Horse
This is a Sticker Page
Complete the following tasks!
Rapunzel loves carrying out these small daily actions for Maximus to ensure she gives him the very best care.
1
TRACE and COLOR these apples... Maximus's favorite treat!
2
Gently RUB Maximus's snout to give him a CUDDLE!
3
COLOR the water blue to GIVE Maximus a drink.
4
GIVE him some grain by placing the sticker where shown.
Stick
Horsey Fact
A stable often has a loft where food, such as hay, can be STORED to FEED the horses in the winter.
77

Riding Outfits

It is a lovely **sunny day** in the kingdom of Corona, so Rapunzel and Maximus are getting ready for **another exciting ride** in the countryside.

Stick

Color in Rapunzel and Maximus in their riding outfits!

Find the pictures on the **sticker sheet** and use them to **guide** you.

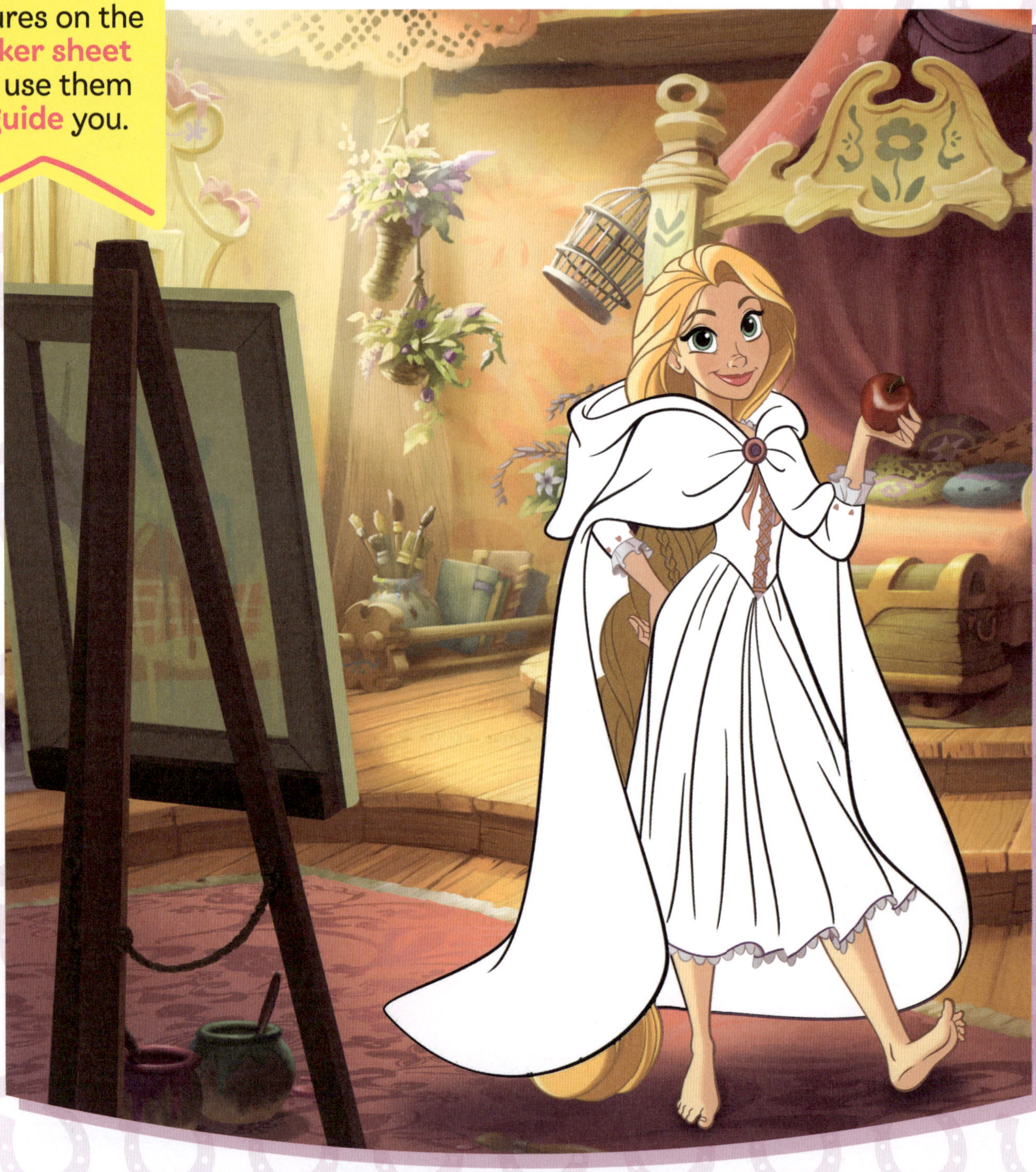

Stick

Horsey Fact

It is important to **TIE YOUR HAIR BACK** so it does not get blown in your face when you are riding along!

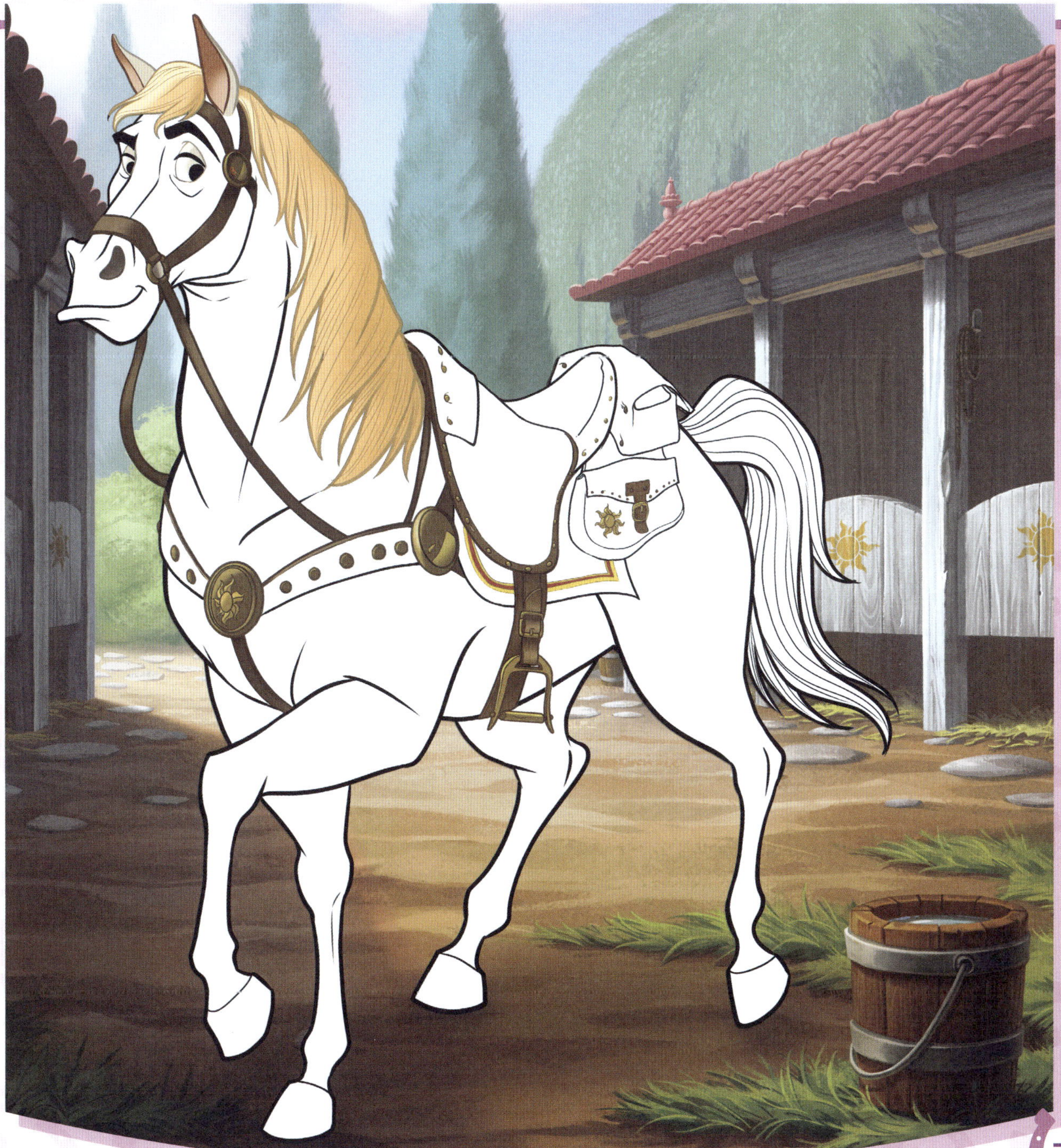

Pearl and Ariel

Pearl is **beautiful** and so **loving**. She enjoys **being around people** and is extremely **charming**. She has lots of **energy** and **loves** searching for treasures on the beach with Ariel.

Pearl the Egyptian Arabian

ORIGIN: Egyptian Arabian horses descend from the fine horses bred by the **Bedouin** people, who were among the very first people to live and travel with them.

FEATURES: They have a **dished face** with a **refined muzzle**. When their **ears** are **upright** and **forward**, some form the shape of a heart.

ATTITUDE: Egyptian Arabian horses are **loyal**, **intelligent**, and **friendly**. Because of their intelligence, they have a **good memory** and **learn quickly**.

Look at all the treasures Ariel and Pearl have found on the beach! **Check** them **off** as you spot each one in the picture.

Color in the blank parts to complete the picture. **Use** this picture to **guide** you.

Solution

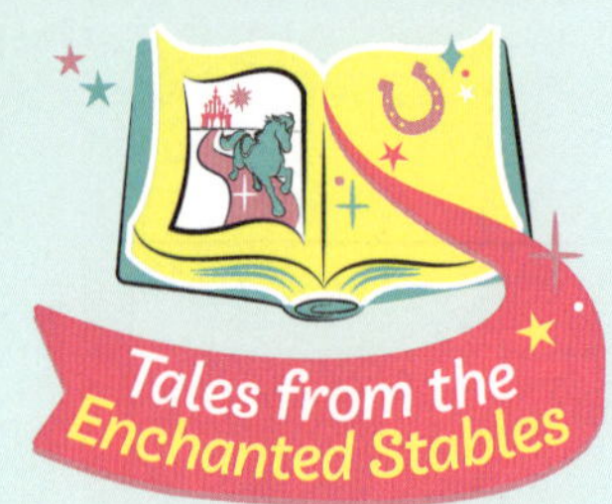

A Day Out

Pearl is a **caring** and **kind** horse, and today she has arranged a **special moment** for Ariel. Read all about it in this charming tale.

Script: Harriet Webster for Book on a Tree; layout: Benedetta Barone; cleanup: Marco Colletti; color: Maawillustration; lettering: Maurizio Clausi for Symmaceo; comics editing: Valentina Cambi

MAYBE A RIDE WILL HELP...
LOOKS LIKE YOU TWO HAD THE SAME IDEA!

ALL RIGHT. LET'S GO!
SEE YOU LATER, TOM!
NEIGH!

OUT OF THE STABLES...
SO WHERE ARE WE GOING?

LATER...
AH, THAT IS WHERE WE ARE GOING...
TO THE BEACH!
CLOP
CLOP

SMELL THAT OCEAN AIR, PEARL!
SNIFF

I HAVE MISSED THE SEA!
SPLASH

SWISH

AND I MISSED YOU!
SCUTTLE?!
FLAP
FLAP

WE MISSED YOU, TOO!

I MISSED YOU ALL!

WELL, ARE YOU READY?

FOR WHAT?

YOUR PARTY!

A FEW YEARS AGO, ON THIS DAY...
YOU BECAME A HUMAN!
OH, I ALMOST FORGOT!

WE GOT YOU A PRESENT!

MY DINGLEHOPPER!

NO, IT IS A FORK!
NEIGH!
HAHA!

The End

Pearls of the Ocean

Ariel and Pearl live in a **beautiful castle** that overlooks the ocean. Ariel adores **collecting** beautiful **shells, seaflowers,** and **oyster shells** as she strolls along the beach with Pearl.

Decorate Pearl's tail and mane with **stickers.** Don't forget to **dress** Ariel for the ride, too.

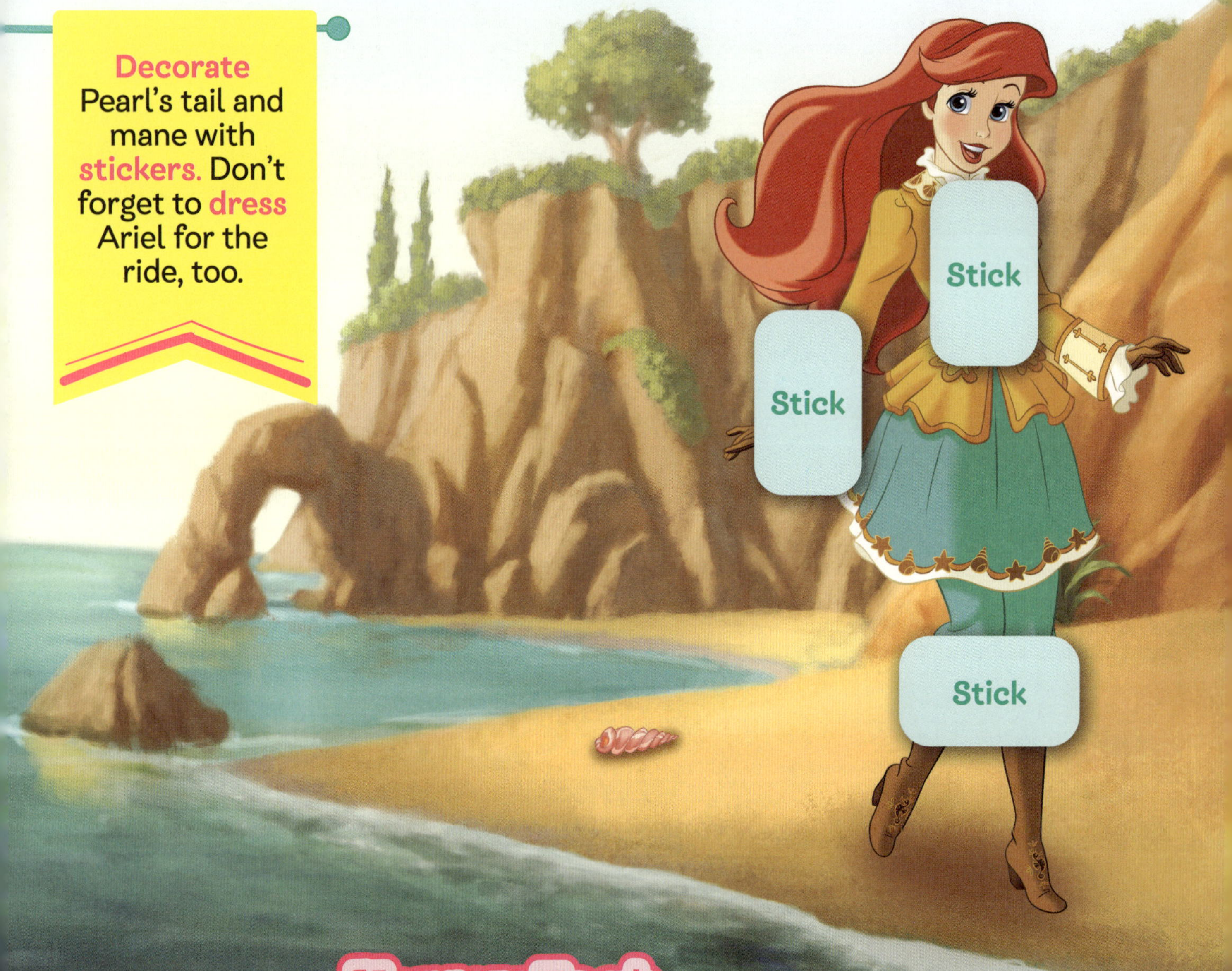

Stick

Stick

Stick

Horsey Fact

RUNNING along the **BEACH** is very useful for racehorses. Training on the sand is low impact because the **SAND** is **SOFT,** and the **SEAWATER** can soothe a horse's skin, **CLEANING** cuts and **LOOSENING** muscles.

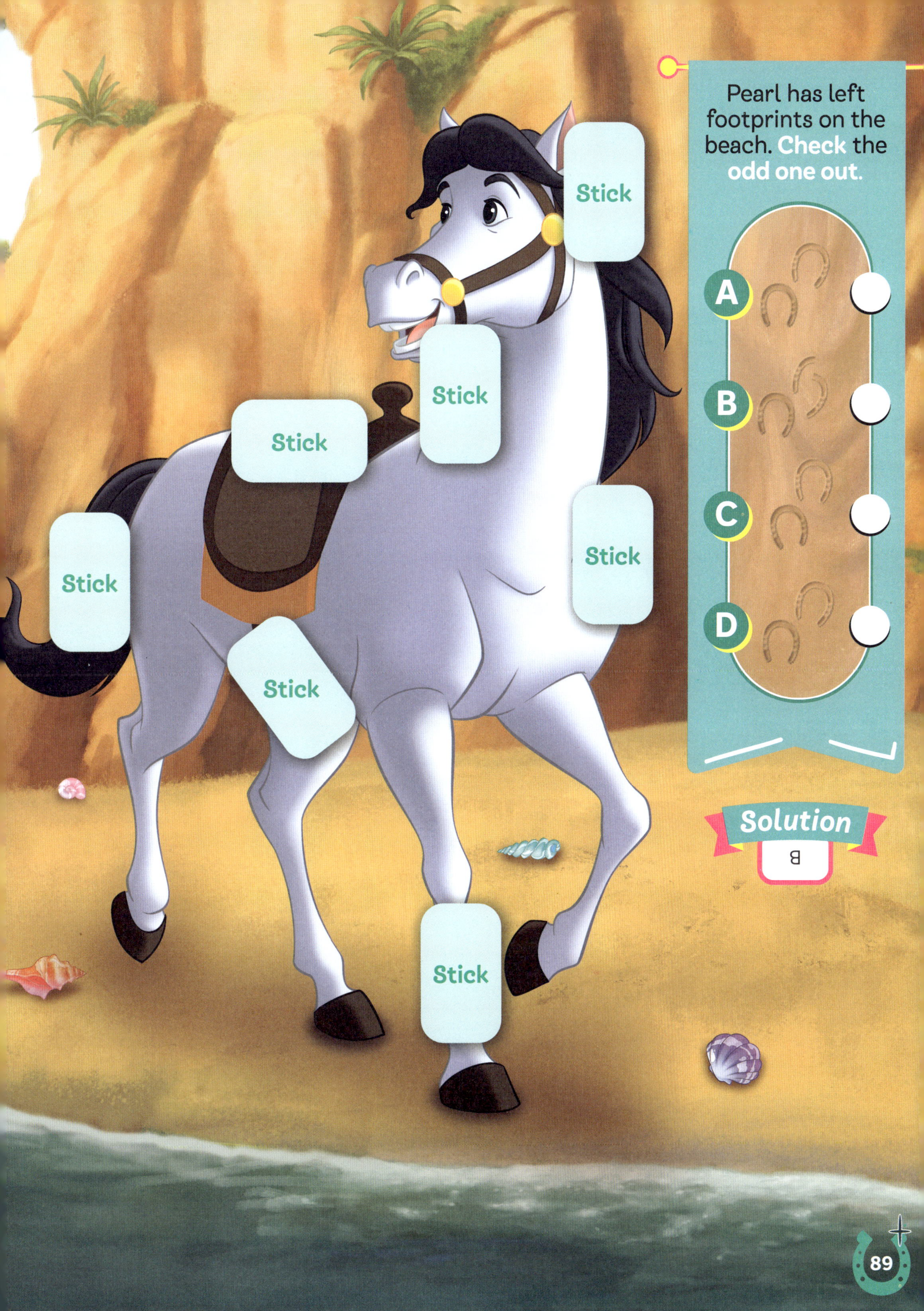
Stick
Stick
Stick
Stick
Stick
Stick
Stick
Pearl has left footprints on the beach. Check the odd one out.
A
B
C
D
Solution
B

Feeding Time

Ariel says Pearl is her most precious treasure! She is always ensuring Pearl eats foods that maintain her high energy levels.

Arrange these foods into two groups: foods that are good for Pearl and foods that aren't. Look carefully at the color of the outline to guide you!

Good for Pearl

Bad for Pearl

Horsey Fact

Arabian horses **DON'T NEED** to **EAT** as much as other horses their size. Their ancestors came from the **DESERT,** where food was **SCARCE,** and because of this they can be active even with little food available.

Ariel just gave Pearl one of her **favorite foods! Color** the **yellow dotted spaces** below to see what it is.

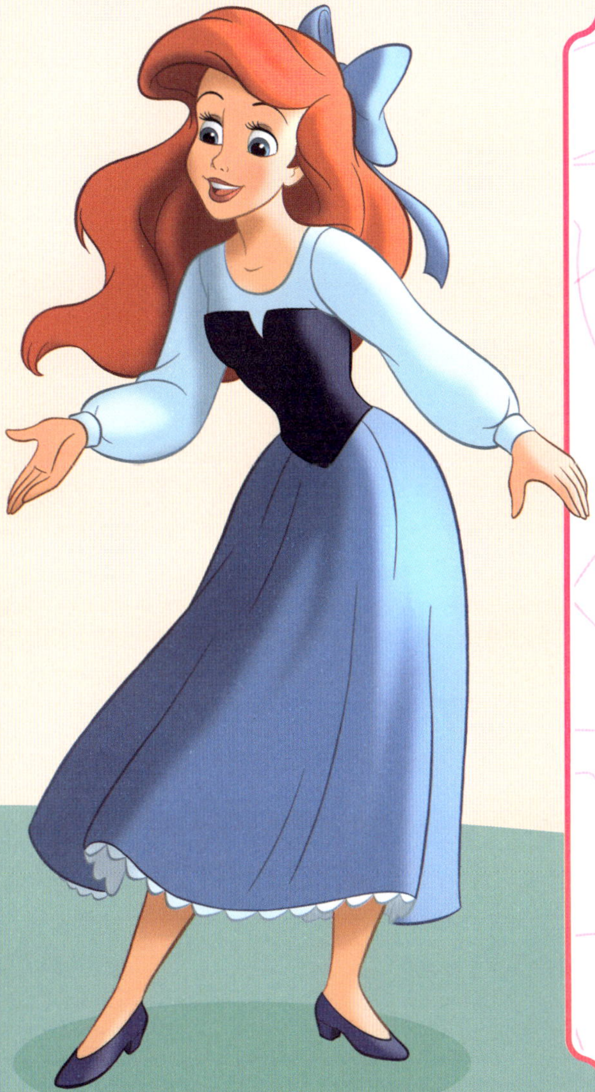

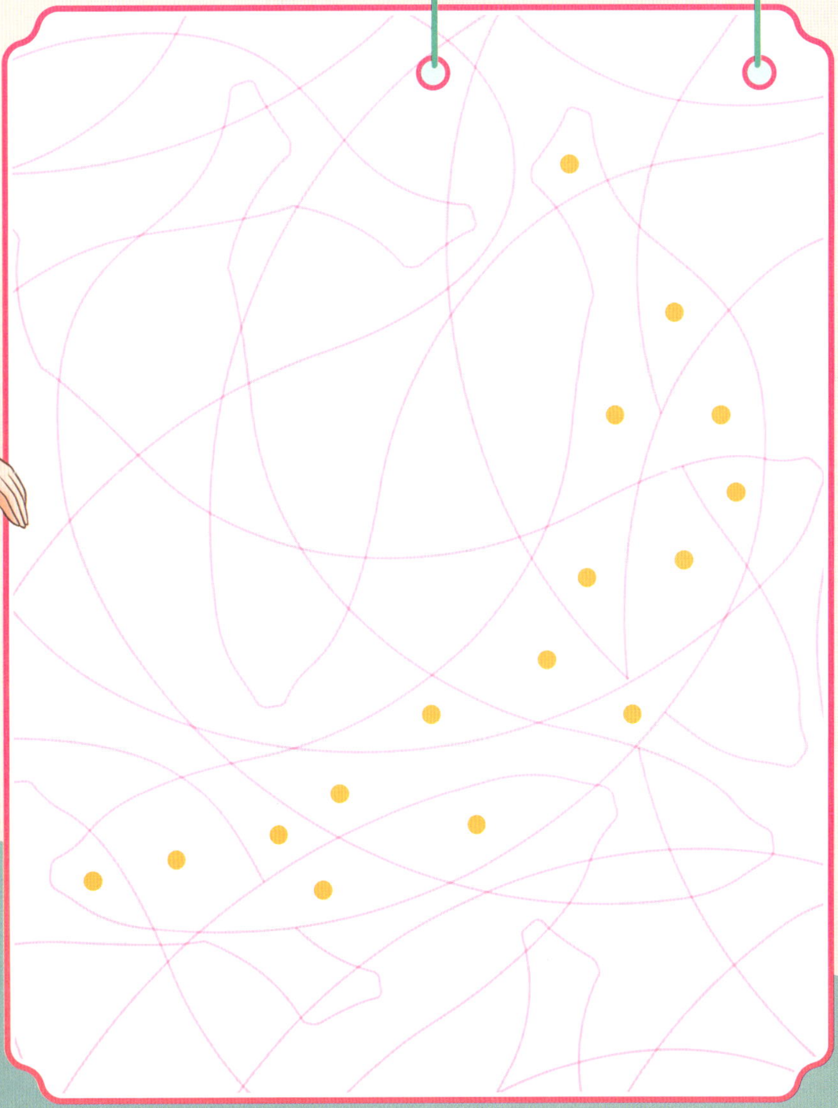

Horse Care Tip

FRUITS such as apples are a **GOOD TREAT** for horses and they are a much **HEALTHIER OPTION** than sugar cubes.

Solutions

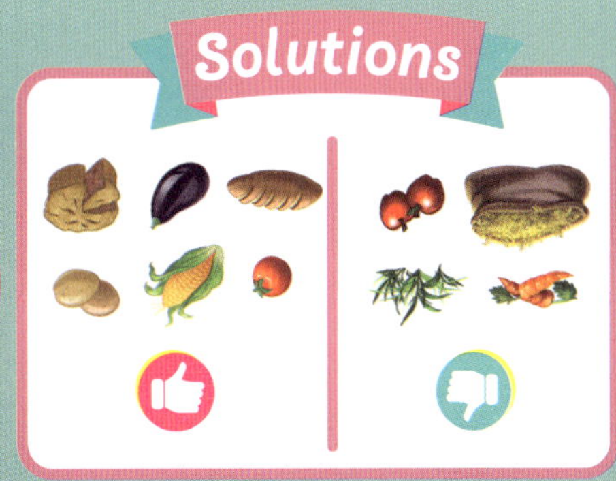

Philippe and Belle

Philippe is trustworthy, strong, and adventurous. He loves his out-of-town trips with Belle, where they ride through the beautiful French countryside together, stopping off here and there. How fun!

Philippe the Belgian Draft Horse

ORIGIN: Breeding of the Belgian draft horse was officially begun in the 17th century in Belgium by the farmers, who used these horses to work on farms.

ATTITUDE: Like other draft horses, the Belgian draft horses are much stronger than other breeds and they are perfect for pulling carriages and wagons.

FEATURES: Typically, their coat color is light chestnut with coppery shades. They also have a flaxen mane and tail.

Point to the tallest sunflower!

Solution
C

An Unexpected Surprise

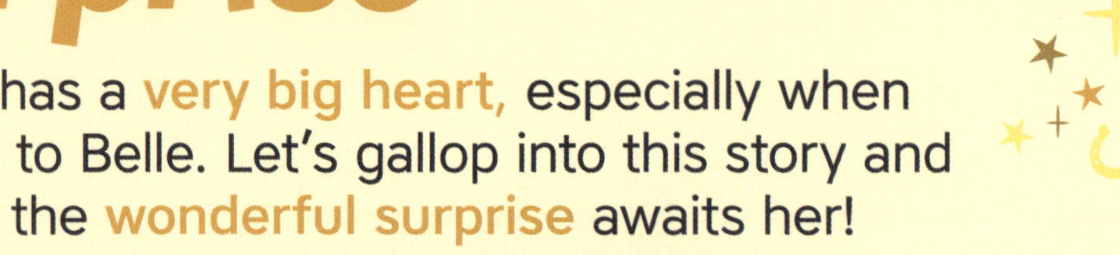

Philippe has a very big heart, especially when it comes to Belle. Let's gallop into this story and discover the wonderful surprise awaits her!

BELLE AND PHILIPPE FINISH A STORY...

"... AND THE BRAVE PRINCESS DEFEATS THE EVIL WIZARD!"

THE END.

Script: Harriet Webster for Book on a Tree; layout, cleanup and ink: Marino Gentile; color: Maawillustration; lettering: Maurizio Clausi for Symmaceo

IN THE WOODS...
WHERE ARE WE GOING?
NEIGH!

OKAY, I TRUST YOU, PHILIPPE!

CLIP
CLOP

A LITTLE LATER...
PHEW! WE ARE OUT OF THE WOODS!
HMM, WHAT IS OVER THERE?

WAIT!

IT IS A BOOKSTORE!
Bookstore

THANK YOU, PHILIPPE!

I WILL BE RIGHT BACK...

WELL, MAYBE LONGER!

WOW! I COULD SPEND ALL DAY IN HERE.
WELCOME! HOW MAY I HELP YOU?

DO YOU HAVE ANY NEW BOOKS?
THESE ARRIVED TODAY!

I DID NOT HAVE TIME...
TO PUT THEM ON THE SHELVES YET!
DO YOU HAVE ANY MORE?

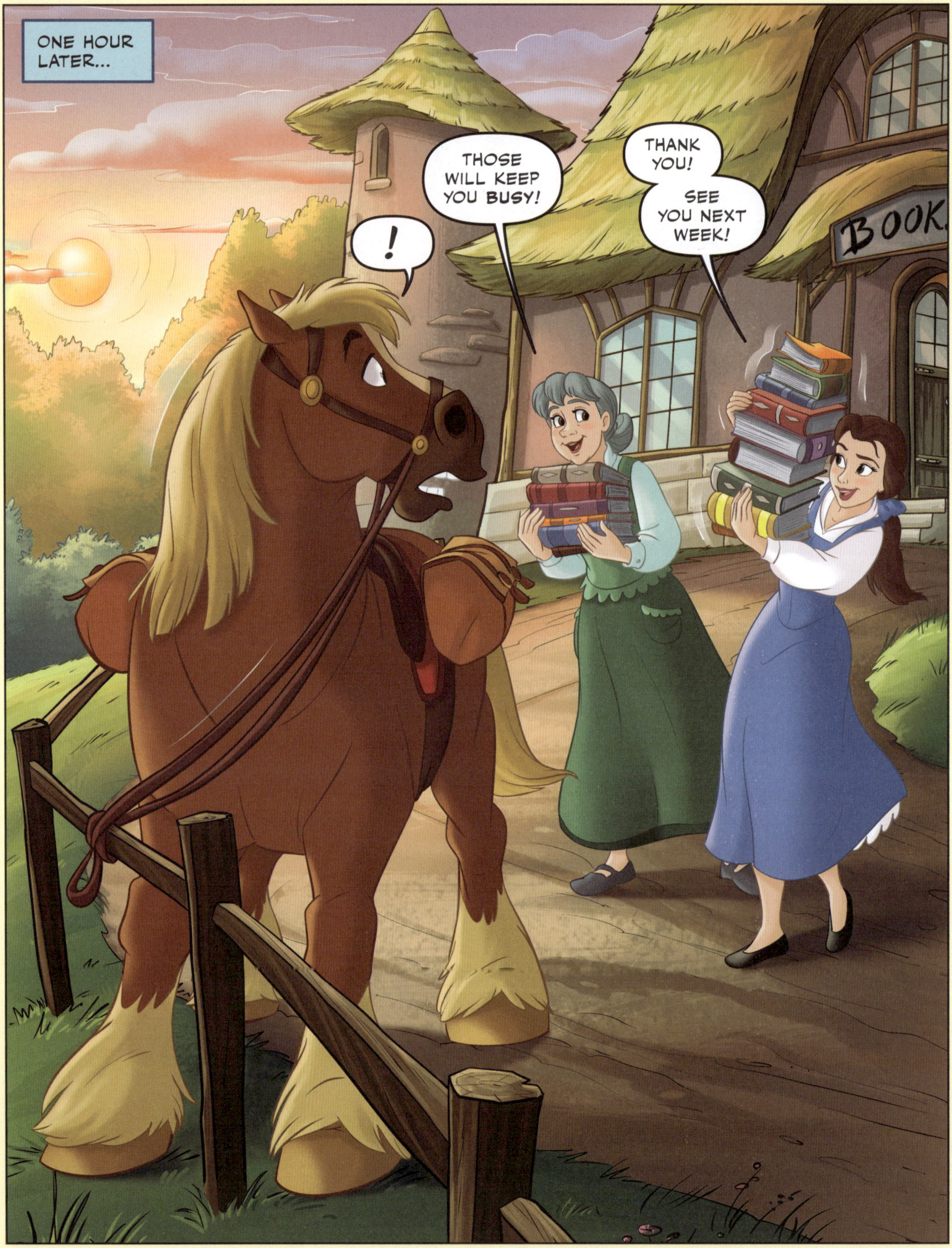

ONE HOUR LATER...

!

THOSE WILL KEEP YOU **BUSY**!

THANK YOU!

SEE YOU NEXT WEEK!

The End

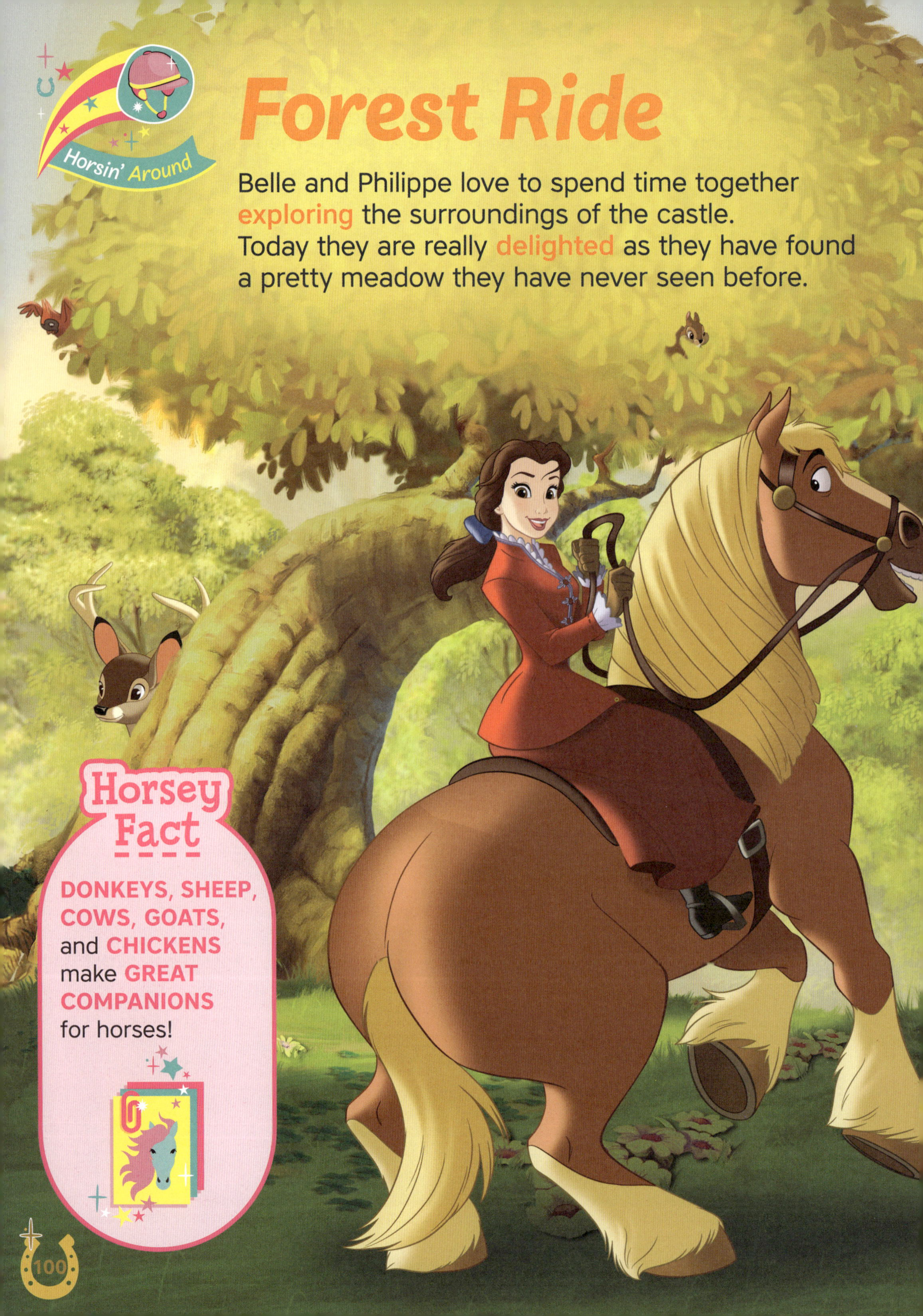

Forest Ride

Belle and Philippe love to spend time together exploring the surroundings of the castle. Today they are really delighted as they have found a pretty meadow they have never seen before.

Horsey Fact

DONKEYS, SHEEP, COWS, GOATS, and **CHICKENS** make **GREAT COMPANIONS** for horses!

Which **animals** do Belle and Philippe encounter on their ride?
Match the right sticker with each shadow in the box.
Then **look closely** at the picture and **spot** them all!
Stick
Stick
Stick
Stick
Stick
Stick
Solutions
Horsey Fact
Horses can be **SPOOKED** by spiders, butterflies, or birds mainly because they **MOVE QUICKLY** out of hidden spaces!
This is a Sticker Page

Horsin' Around

Following Philippe's Nose

Belle and Philippe adore visiting the bustling French markets near their village. And this morning Philippe has sniffed out all the delicious food stalls in no time at all!

Follow the trail and answer the questions along the way.

Use the number line to help you when counting!

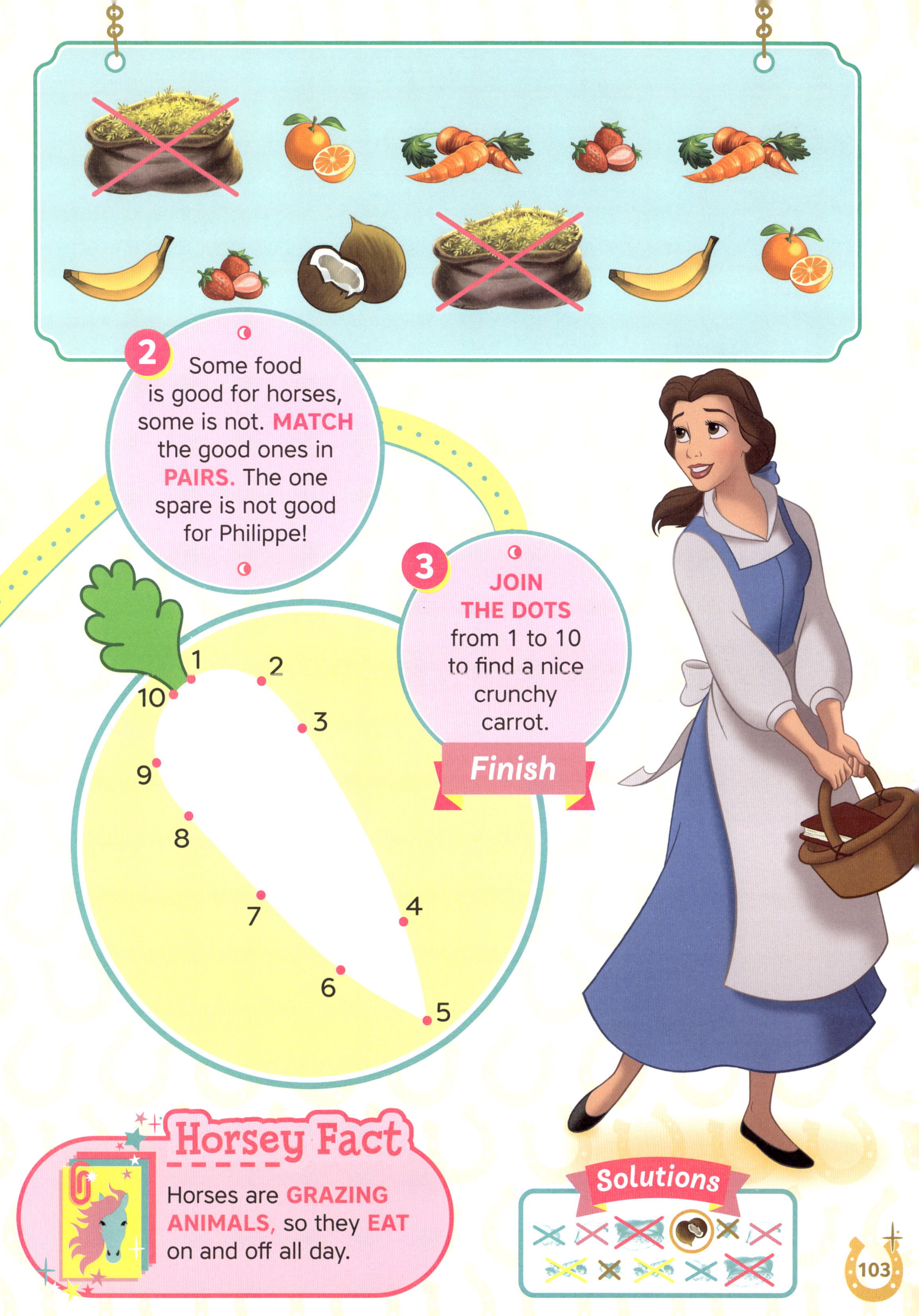

2
Some food is good for horses, some is not. **MATCH** the good ones in **PAIRS.** The one spare is not good for Philippe!
3
JOIN THE DOTS from 1 to 10 to find a nice crunchy carrot.
1
2
3
4
5
6
7
8
9
10
Finish
Horsey Fact
Horses are **GRAZING ANIMALS,** so they **EAT** on and off all day.
Solutions

Major and Cinderella

When Cinderella married the Prince, Major **moved** to the royal stables of the castle, and he is now her **personal horse.** They share many **magical moments together!**

Major the Selle Français

ORIGIN: Selle Français (meaning French saddle horse) is a breed of **sport horse** originally from **France.**

FEATURES: They are usually **bay** or **chestnut** in color but can also be **gray** and **black. White marks** are common, especially on the lower legs.

ATTITUDE: They are **gentle, friendly,** and **eager to please** their owners. They often excel at **show jumping** and do well at **eventing,** a combination of dressage, show jumping, and cross-country jumping.

What does Cinderella always pack when they go for a ride? **Cross out** all the **M**s for Major to find out.

M A M P M P
M M L M E M

A _ _ _ _

Color in the blank parts to complete the picture. **Use** this picture to **guide** you.

Solution

Apple

Major's Moment

Major is gentle, **friendly,** and **cares for others.** During a **woodland adventure** with Cinderella, he proves to be **very brave.** Read all about their ride full of surprises!

Script: Harriet Webster for Book on a Tree; layout and cleanup: Marino Gentile; color: Maawillustration; comics editing: Valentina Cambi; lettering: Maurizio Clausi for Symmaceo

OUCH, YOU STEPPED ON MY PAW!
WHOOSH

HELLO!

HOW NICE! YOU ARE HERE, TOO!
WE WANTED TO SURPRISE YOU!

IT IS TIME TO EAT!

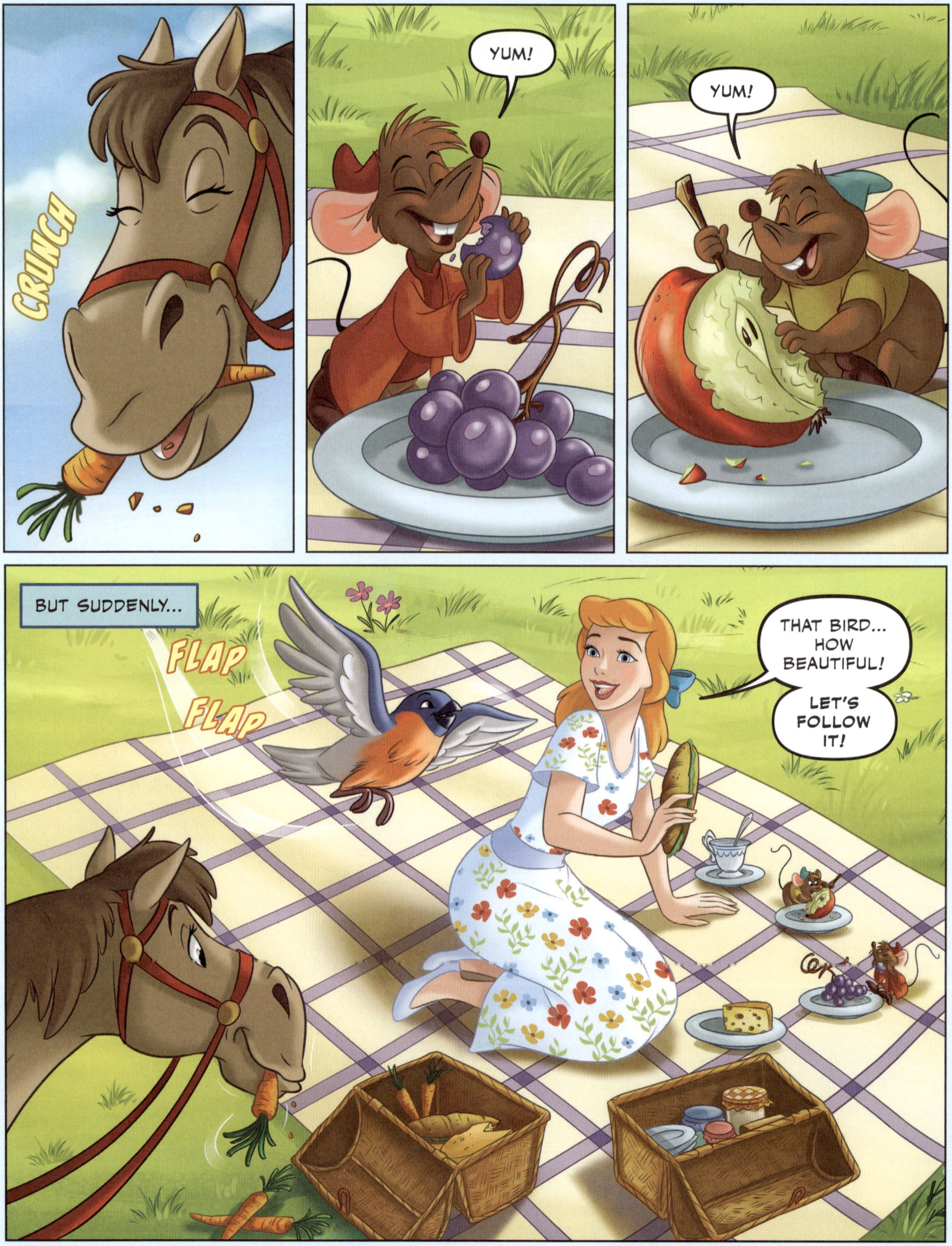

BUT SUDDENLY...

FLAP
FLAP

THAT BIRD... HOW BEAUTIFUL!

LET'S FOLLOW IT!

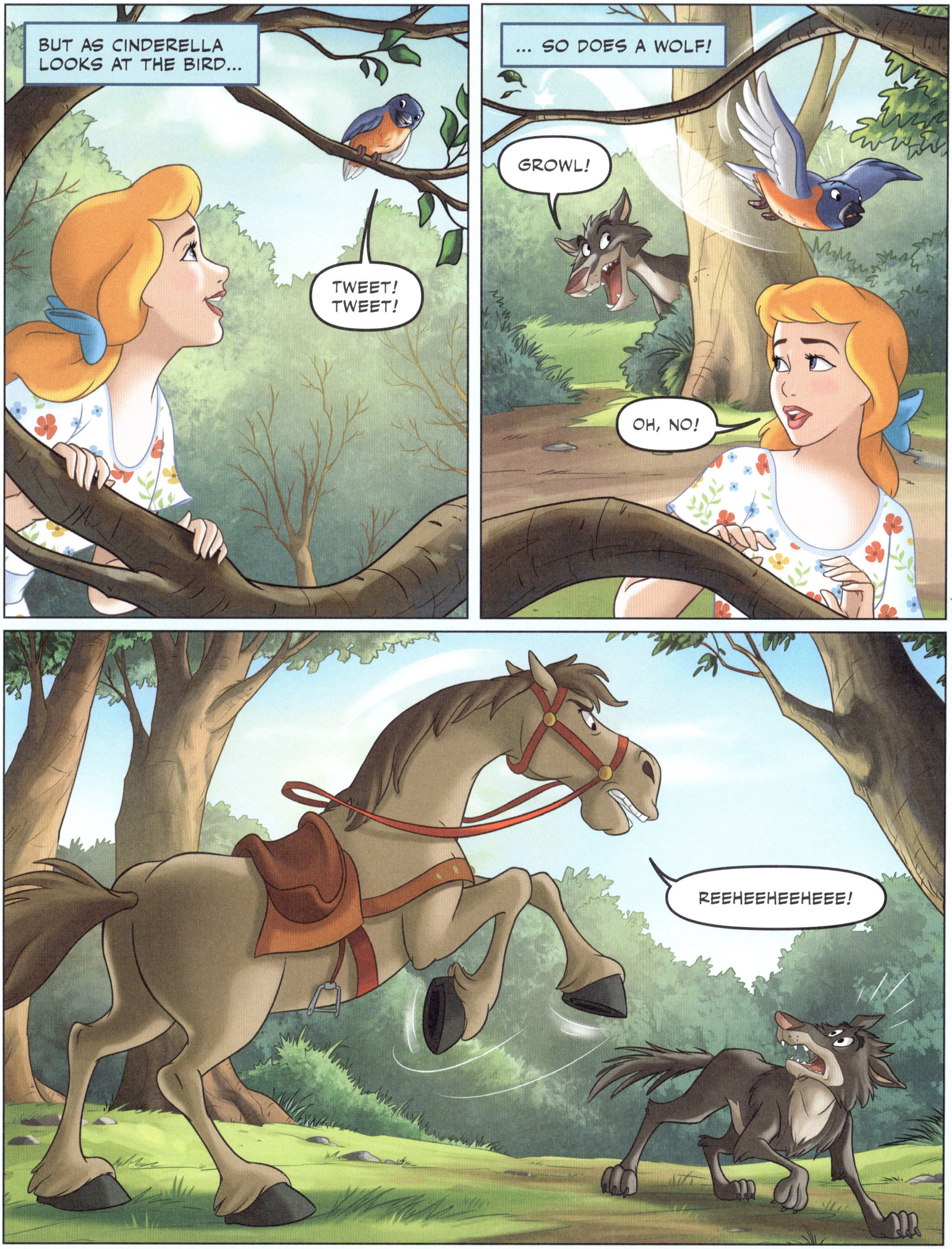

REEHEEHEEHEEE!

MAJOR!

BRBRBRBRBRBRBR!

WOOF?

WHIMPER!
WELL DONE!

NEIGH!

BACK AT THE STABLES...
MAJOR, YOU WERE SO **BRAVE** TODAY!
YES, HE WAS **GREAT**!

I KNOW I CAN ALWAYS COUNT ON YOU!
Major
CLIP
CLOP

I'M LUCKY TO HAVE YOU AS MY **FRIEND**!
WE ARE **LUCKY**, TOO!
The End

Let's Picnic!

Major is a **courageous horse.** Can you complete these activities inspired by the story so he can **share** a lovely **picnic** with Cinderella and the mice?

1 **DRAW AND COLOR** the tree so Cinderella and Major can find a **NICE PLACE** to eat.

2 Can you **SPOT GUS** and **JAQ?**

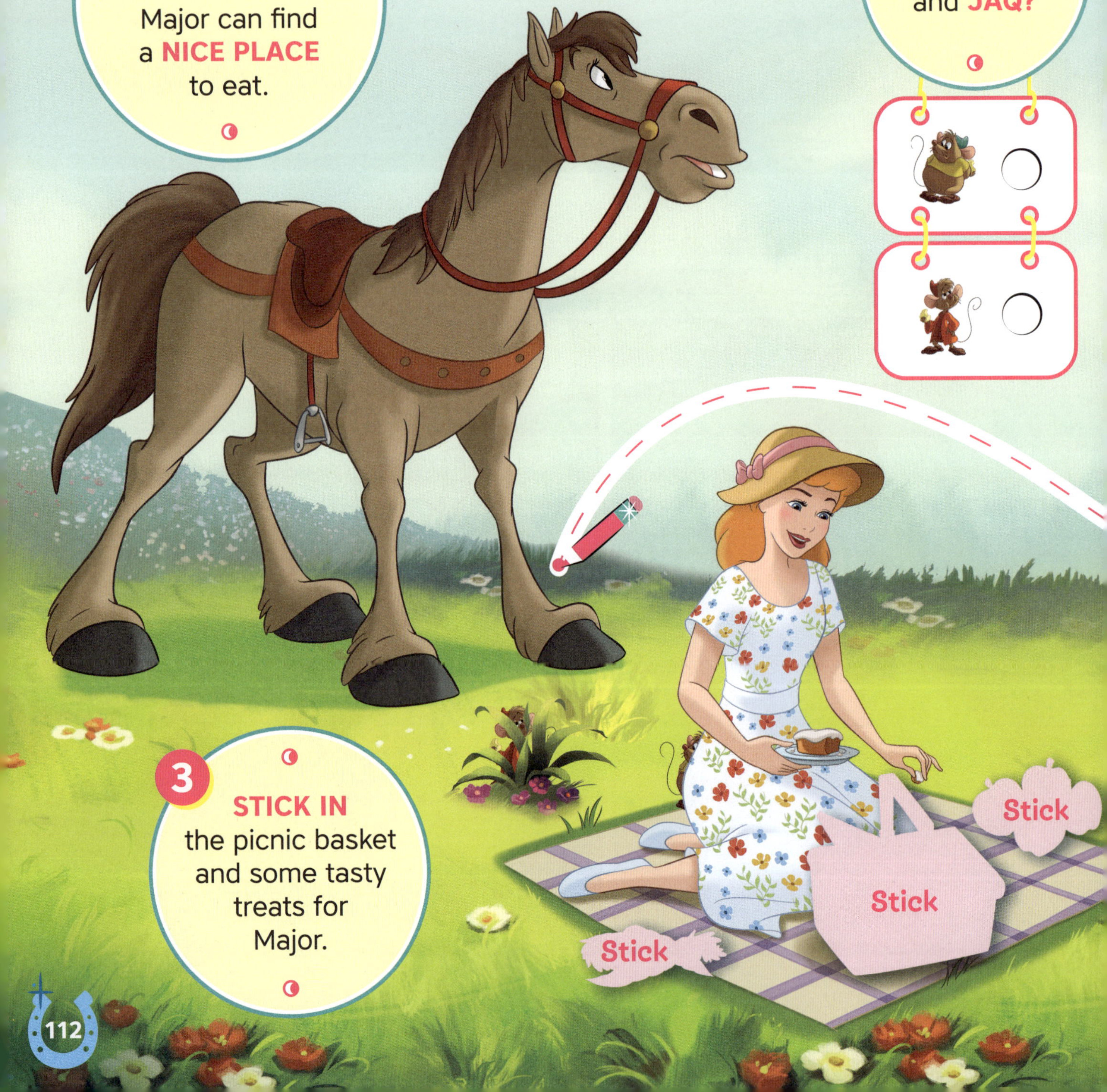

3 **STICK IN** the picnic basket and some tasty treats for Major.

Stick

Stick

Stick

Stick

4
STICK IN
the BULLFINCH
Cinderella is
going to see.

5
Oh, no! It's a wolf!
TRACE THE LINE
so Major can MOVE
FORWARD and
SCARE it away!

Horsey Fact
Some birds like to MAKE
NESTS from discarded
HORSE HAIR!

Solutions

Horsin' Around
Show Jumping
Cinderella and Major often take part in exciting show jumping competitions. Complete the activities on the horse-riding course where they're competing.
1
COLOR
this fence
red and
white.
2
Now
COLOR this
hedge.
Jump!
3
Decide
HOW MANY
jumps Major has
to make here by
DRAWING
them in.

FINISH

Hooray!

6 Congratulations! You have **COMPLETED** the course! **ADD A DESIGN** to the finish flag.

4 A cheering crowd is watching the performance. **TRACE OVER** their exclamation!

Jump!

5 Add an obstacle here. **POP ON** a sticker!

Stick

Jump!

Horsey Fact

In **SHOW JUMPING** the horse and rider try to clear jumps as quickly and cleanly as possible.

Pepper and Tiana

Pepper is **determined** and **hardworking,** just like her friend Tiana. So when it is time for Tiana to take a day off from her restaurant, they cannot wait to go for a **long, relaxing ride** through the bayou.

Pepper the Thoroughbred

ORIGIN: These horses descend from Arabian horses; they originated in England and were developed as perfect sport horses.

FEATURES: They have **long legs** and an **athletic build,** which makes them **superb athletes.** Their average race speed is **35 to 40 miles per hour,** which is the same as the average speed of a car!

ATTITUDE: These horses are **very intelligent, quick to learn,** and **adaptable.** They're also **energetic, bold,** and **spirited,** which makes them better for experienced riders.

Color in the blank parts to complete the picture. **Use** this picture to **guide** you.

Find their **trail** to the bayou.

Pepper's Idea

Pepper is **smart** and **energetic,** and she can be quite **persuasive** when she wants to be. She even manages to get Tiana to take a little break from her cooking duties, with **delicious results!**

Script: Harriet Webster for Book on a Tree; layout and cleanup: Sara Storino; color: Maawillustration; lettering: Maurizio Clausi for Symmaceo; comics editing: Valentina Cambi

HMM.

TOO SWEET!

SIGH! WHAT DO I DO?

NEIGH!
OH, PEPPER, HOW DID YOU GET OUT?

OKAY, JUST A LITTLE RIDE...

SOON AFTER...
WHAT A SUNNY DAY!
CLOP
CLOP

I FEEL BETTER ALREADY!

PEPPER? WHAT HAVE YOU FOUND?

CHOMP

OH, MAYHAW BERRIES!
TICK

HMM!

SOUR, BUT TASTY!

PERFECT FOR MY RECIPE...
CLEVER, PEPPER!

LET'S GRAB SOME!
PLOP

BACK IN THE KITCHEN...
HERE GOES...
PLOP
PLOP
PLOP

HISS

THAT NIGHT AFTER THE PARTY...
HEY, PEPPER!

THANKS TO YOU, MAMA LOVED HER PIE...

... SO I SAVED YOU SOME BERRIES!

ENJOY!
CHOMP

The End

Pepper's Special Ingredient

Tiana has a busy day planned in the kitchen. She found some mayhaw berries on her last ride with Pepper and is going to bake a very special pie.

1 **ADD** stickers with essential kitchen tools and ingredients!

2 **HOW MANY** berries does Tiana want to **ADD** to the pie filling? **COUNT** them on the table!

12

Stick

Stick

These are Sticker Pages
Horsey Fact
Every Thoroughbred horse in the Northern Hemisphere HAS THE SAME BIRTHDAY, January 1! This happens to make it easier for owners to KEEP TRACK of HORSES' AGES and enter them in different races by age group.
3
SPOT the WOODEN SPOON Tiana needs to STIR the pie filling.
4
Finish making the pie by COLORING it.
Stick
Solution
Use the number line to help you when counting!
1 2 3 4 5 6 7 8 9 10 11 12

Dressage Practice

Complete these trail activities and remember: practice makes perfect!

Tiana and Pepper are training for a prestigious dressage competition in New Orleans. They are both highly talented, hardworking, and determined, so they should do very well.

Practice this serpentine line!

Change of pace. Go fast and slow as you trace the line.

Horsey Fact

Dressage is the performance of carefully controlled movements that show a **HORSE'S OBEDIENCE, ATHLETIC ABILITY,** and **BALANCE.** It's the result of **TEAMWORK** between horse and rider.

Horse Play
GOOD BALANCE is key in dressage! Practice by WALKING AROUND with an object like a beanbag on your head.
Ride in a circle. Trace the line.
Now it's time for a controlled canter: balance steps evenly!

Saddle Up Quiz!

What **kind of rider** are you?
Take this **"Would You Rather?"** quiz to find out.

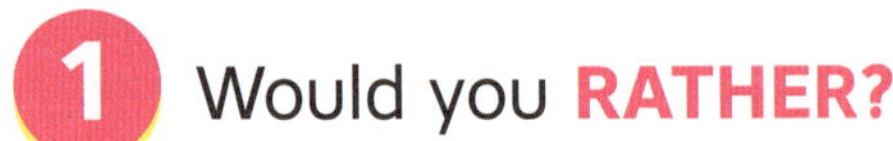

1 Would you **RATHER?**

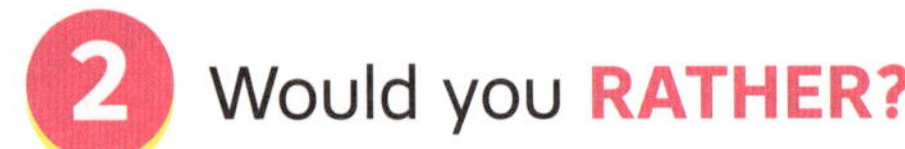

2 Would you **RATHER?**

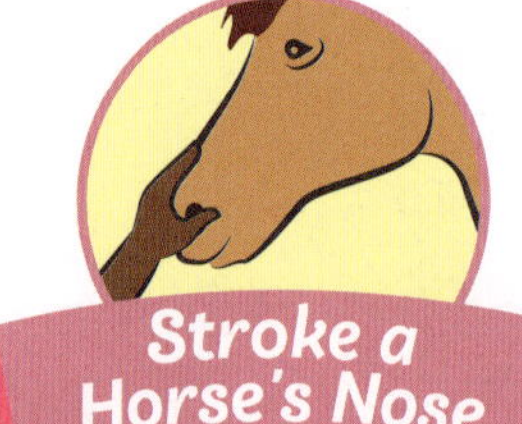

3 Would you **RATHER?**

4 Would you **RATHER GO FOR A RIDE** on a...?

5 Would you **RATHER?**

6 Would you **RATHER GIVE** a horse...?

Mostly Pink

ROMANTIC

You are a **romantic rider** who loves to trot off into the sunset with your horsey pal, taking in all the views!

Mixed

EASYGOING

You **enjoy both** the **adventure** and **romance** of an exhilarating ride with your dearest horse friend!

Mostly Turquoise

ADVENTUROUS

You are an **adventurous rider** who loves setting off on bold and daring adventures with your trusty steed!

P. 4
PP. 16–17
P. 19
P. 4
PP. 30–31

P. 5
PP. 40-41
P. 5
P. 55

P. 5
P. 67
P. 6
P. 77
PP. 78–79
© Disney

P. 6
PP. 88-89
P. 6
P. 100

P. 7
PP. 112–113
P. 115
P. 7
PP. 124–125